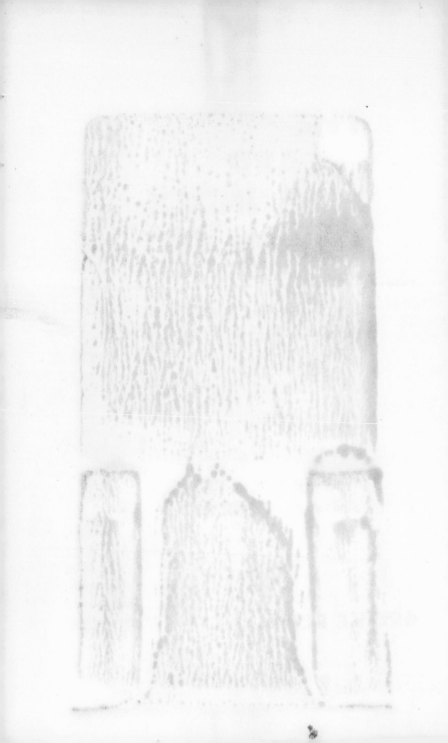

THE
CARD
INDEX
AND OTHER PLAYS

• •

BY TADEUSZ ROZEWICZ

TRANSLATED BY
ADAM CZERNIAWSKI

GROVE PRESS, INC. NEW YORK

111029

Library of Congress Catalog Card Number: 74-101390
First Evergreen Edition, 1970
First Printing
Manufactured in the United States of America

CONTENTS

· ·

THE INTERRUPTED ACT   V

THE CARD INDEX   33

GONE OUT   71

iii

THE INTERRUPTED ACT

THE AUTHOR'S CONFESSION

I spent July and August in town. I did not succumb to the vacation mania. I spent the summer of the century working at the bench. The thermometer was climbing to 40°, 45°, 46° Centigrade. The town was white with heat, quiet and deserted. In such an atmosphere I began to write my first comedy. I intended it to be a bedroom farce. Contemporary. Even at times modern. With the aid of various pseudo-avant-garde tricks the classics are being murdered on the stages of our theaters. This will not do as a substitute for a contemporary theater. Still, this is not the place to criticize the shortcomings of our theater. Let me get back to home ground. And the fact is that my work on *The Interrupted Act* did not result in the fulfillment of my idea. Only the first and second scenes were written according to the original conception. The succeeding two scenes were an act of capitulation. Although in the stage directions I explain the role of the STRANGER I have not been able to work this scene into the plot. Perhaps there was a place for pantomime in this scene. Although when writing the first two scenes I was "decided," when I came to write the third and fourth I lost my self-confidence, my enthusiasm and sense of well-being. In its present form my play is not destined for either the theater or television or radio. The great number of remarks, intrusions, theoretical deliberations, and polemics (with possible opponents) tend to turn this comedy into a narrative script. It may be that dramatists happier than I will be able to make use of the ideas contained in the stage directions (and the polemical remarks) of this play. They mustn't be misled by the playful form in which I present certain formulations concerning the role upon the stage of dialogue, or words, of silence, gesture, and time. It may be that our critics and theorists of the theater (drama) will wish one day to take up the work which was begun before the war by Witkiewicz and Chwistek.* Our theater—or rather, Polish contemporary plays—is based on the "dramaturgy" of the so-called drawing-room flirtation. Various characters tied by all sorts of bonds exchange opinions regarding their various experiences, feelings, and so on. It's enough to read Chwistek's "Theater of the Future," an essay which appeared in *Zwrotnica* in 1922 (!). Anyway, I am addressing myself only to the few "just men." Our theater (our drama) is not bad because it is "modern," it is bad because it is faceless. It is a theater lacking both purpose and ideas. It will not be long before we shall see *Pan Tadeusz, Pan Balcer in Brazil, The Peasants,*† and so on adapted for our largest (and smallest) stages. I am not a typical dramatic author, I am rather a man "approaching the theater." I think, however, that my suggestions (my mistakes and my achievements) may halt the decline of ambition which characterizes our theater repertory in the forthcoming season. Adaptations of "Little Red Riding Hood" or of the telephone directory and the torturing of our classics will not create a contemporary Polish theater. Despite the "enthusiasm" of foreign visitors our theater lacks its own image. Is it not worth thinking and talking about this?

October 8, 1963

---

* Stanislaw Witkiewicz (1885–1939), painter, dramatist, novelist, and philosopher. His plays are now seen as early important manifestations of the theater of the absurd. He experimented with the effects of drugs. He committed suicide when he felt that civilization was coming to an end in September, 1939. Leon Chwistek (1884–1944), philosopher, mathematician, poet, painter, created the Formist theory in art.—*Tr.*

† Respectively the celebrated epic by Adam Mickiewicz, a versified novel by Maria Konopnicka, and a vast novel of peasant life by Wladyslaw Reymont.—*Tr.*

CHARACTERS

CIVIL ENGINEER, FATHER *of the* BEAUTIFUL GIRL

NURSE

BEAUTIFUL GIRL, *daughter of the* ENGINEER

ROBUST WOMAN, HOUSEKEEPER *in the Engineer's house*

STRANGER

FIRST DEPUTY, *the Engineer's deputy*

FIRST WORKER
SECOND WORKER } *from the bridge-building crew*

STAGE DIRECTIONS
AND REMARKS

The stage represents a large room. The door on the left leads to the right and the door on the right leads to the left. There is also a door in the third (middle) wall. The room contains furniture and pictures completely devoid of character. Three white hairs, not visible from the auditorium, are lying on a shelf. Two, perhaps three, flies buzz around the room but they will not play any significant role in the development of the action.

A beautiful shapely GIRL *holding a big suitcase walks across the room. She has just said goodbye to her* FATHER, *a well-known* CIVIL ENGINEER, *and is leaving forever to go to America, to the family of her dead mother. Her* FATHER *is not seeing her off because he is lying in his study on a divan with his leg in a plaster cast. It is his left leg. We cannot, alas, prove on the stage—with the help of "theatrical" means—that the* GIRL *is leaving forever or even that she is leaving for North America. We are helpless. True, we could employ a narrator, a telephone, the Father's voice coming from the next room, but all these are very primitive half-measures. One could just as well be going off (with a suitcase) to college, on vacation, or out to take one's washing to the laundry. True, the* FATHER *could have cried out, "As soon as you land in America, let me know," but he would have had to add, for example, "in North America." Using the telephone the* GIRL *might make inquiries about air connections with Hamburg, Lisbon, and New York. Alas, all this has already taken place before the curtain rose and the* GIRL *is crossing the room in a quite ordinary way although she is on her way to America. The Girl's*

3

FATHER *is enjoying a well-earned convalescence and holiday. A week earlier, under his supervision, the last cofferdam under the last pillar of the last span was filled with concrete. Work on the construction of the longest bridge linking east-central Europe with southwest Europe took ten years. Last week teams of workers met in the middle of the bridge. We provide these considerable details of the worthy Engineer's achievement because we are unable to present on the stage the gigantic enterprise, the failures, the achievements and frustrations which accompanied the* ENGINEER *and the crew in building the bridge. Like an (almost) vulgar realist I did indeed ponder the possibility of placing the first scene in the draftsman's office or in the foreman's cabin in the middle of the works, of (possibly) showing the construction of (at least) a sector, a pillar, a span, of showing the moment when the* ENGINEER *slipped and fell into the water. His cry. Of the clinic in which they set his left leg and put it in a plaster cast. His conversation with the pretty* NURSE. *I could even show the Engineer's youth by making use of the medical registrar who was the renowned hero's (I am not afraid of this word) schoolmate. I came to the conclusion, however, that all these scenes would have taken about forty-five minutes, while during that time the actual "drama" might have completed its course. In his room the* ENGINEER *is in fact experiencing a great drama but, alas, this we cannot see. Had I transported the action into the Engineer's study I would not have achieved any stage effect because he is a very reserved man. It may be that at this very moment he is breaking down or even has broken down, but we are not able to show this internal struggle because we lack the external means. Various types of facial expressions, gestures, or even cries are not "capable of" representing the suffering. Naturally, one could dispose of all this with the aid of dialogue, but it is a singularly vulgar and base method. Even a monologue would be better. But in order to explain the whole tangle of tragic events one would have needed twenty minutes and again the action would have suffered terribly. He could have told the audience, "I am suffering," but the fact*

4

that a young girl with a suitcase has left home does not justify a man's suffering, and some of the audience would (in any event) gain the impression that the ENGINEER *is suffering on account of his leg being in a cast. Alas, we have no time to show in our theater (through pictures and dialogue) the causes that led to the young person's departure, although in this instance I have yielded to temptation and I will show a little scene in which lies the seed, the cause of the drama (or rather, the departure) of the young person. For the time being let's return to the stage. If during her passage across the stage the* GIRL *had turned her head and said "Bye-bye, Daddy, farewell, Father, goodbye," etc., the whole case would immediately have blossomed out and made dramatic sense. Alas, the* GIRL *has uttered these and many other words in her Father's study. When she passes across the stage she has already done with all "farewells." She can, of course, turn back. Let's say she picks up the key to the door. Since this key will not be of any use to her (in America) she takes it back to her* FATHER. *This shows that the situation in contemporary theater is difficult and at times has no solution. I have of course in mind the one realistic theater worthy of the name—poetic theater. And it's not enough to perform trepanations on* The Forefathers *and* Mazeppa.* *It's not enough to have grotesque student jokes. Even our stage designers are helpless. Only a new realistico-poetic theater may open—not the door, I don't say that—but a chink in the door leading to the exit. In this case we do not disdain minute details, small, even microscopic, stage props (which cannot be seen from the auditorium), we do not disdain information contained in the stage directions. On the contrary, I want to use this information as a spring of the whole "show." (At the moment I have, alas, no better definition.) Stage directions must be included in the theater program. They are as important for my theater as instruments are for a surgeon during an operation (naturally). They are even*

---

* Two well-known plays by Adam Mickiewicz and Juliusz Slowacki respectively.—*Tr.*

more important than my biography, a list of my plays, first nights, prizes, stage productions, and other similar elements of a purely decorative nature. My theater is a living organism. It resembles a man, an invalid, who lost his left leg in battle but continues to feel pain in that leg. For this theater has lost its dramatic action (that structure which was the goal of the efforts of Greek, Elizabethan, and to some extent Warsaw and even Crakow dramatists), but this lost essential member continues to cause me pain. Sometimes in moments of weakness and despair I make use of this long-lost left leg (action) and then I resemble certain foreign and native dramatists. But giving to Witkiewicz what belongs to Witkiewicz and to Gombrowicz what belongs to Witkiewicz, I wish to declare that as far as I am concerned they are both authors of classics. Great writers who have taken their place next to Slowacki, Norwid, Krasinski, Wyspianski, Fredro, Zapolska, Chwistek, and others. I bow to all these great ones and pass on. I say nothing about "the young" because one never knows how they will end up. Following this (polemical) interlude, which however throws a certain light on my stagecraft and its (hidden) roots, I proceed to complete the recording of my stage directions. After the young GIRL, *who is (probably) the daughter of the* ENGINEER *lying in the study, has left the room, the stage is empty. One of the three flies (which I mentioned at the beginning of these remarks) buzzes across the room and alights on a lump of sugar. I forgot to add that on the table there is a sugar bowl filled with lumps of sugar. After a pause which, depending on the producer and the critic, may last anywhere from one to five minutes (the five-minute pause may be used only in the case of either a very sophisticated or a completely unsophisticated audience)—after a pause, then a* WOMAN *slowly walks across the stage. She is carrying a pair of well-pressed men's trousers. These trousers may be cream, blue, or gray, with cuffs. The width of the leg at the cuff is twenty-nine to thirty-four centimeters. At the moment of her appearance on the stage the* WOMAN *is sixty. She has smoothly combed black hair,*

*a slightly shriveled face, and an ordinary dress lacking character
and shape. The* WOMAN *stops by the table with the sugar bowl.
She chases the fly away. She glances at the trousers. She scratches
at a stain which (from the auditorium) is invisible. She hangs the
trousers on the back of one of the four chairs which stand around
the table. She takes a lump of sugar out of the sugar bowl and
puts it in her mouth. She sucks the sugar. This action deforms
her cheeks and lips to some extent. The* WOMAN *is listening to
find out whether anyone is moving next door. She stands thus for
almost sixty seconds. She then goes out by the middle door, which
she leaves ajar (not wide open but only ajar). There is a click and
the sound of a key in the lock. Apparently someone has entered
the hall. Through the door left ajar we can hear him taking off
his coat. It is a stiff green waterproof oilskin or tarpaulin. (But
this we shall not be able to see on the stage during the course of
the play.) The person who has entered splutters like a wet cat.
A shower must have caught him in the street but we cannot be
certain of this. Forty-five seconds after the* WOMAN *has left, a
gray-haired* MAN *in a dark suit enters the room. He takes a
handkerchief out of his pocket and wipes either his whole face or
just his mouth. His actions are very free, he feels "very much
at home" (or maybe even better). He sits on one of the chairs.
The* WOMAN *must have told him that the host is still asleep. The
guest has decided to wait. He looks around the room. He walks
up to the cabinet or sideboard (possibly a bar) and pours himself
a glass of brandy. He drinks appreciatively. He sits at the table.
He is scrutinizing his left hand, or rather his fingernails. Then
his eyes move to his foot, shod in a black patent-leather shoe. He
examines his black sock with a red stripe. Rubs his brow with
his hand. This scene may last one to three minutes and in favor-
able circumstances even seven. This* MAN, *who in five days' time
will be forty-two, has only twenty-four hours ago been released
from prison and fully reinstated. He is rather pale, but this pallor
could also be the result of the previous day's drinking. Our play
still hasn't begun and it is difficult at this moment to foresee when*

7

it will. But, after all, I do know it will start the moment the first word is uttered. For in the beginning of the contemporary theater there was, there is, and there will be, the word. An instrument of communication so imperfect and yet irreplaceable. Primitive and indispensable. Like water, devoid of taste but essential to life. As a realist writer I strive, however, that the word in my theater should not have a larger meaning than it has in life. The MAN *in the business suit stays in the room for a while longer. He drinks the brandy and leaves. Apparently didn't wish to wake the host. Admittedly he had certain urgent business to transact with the host, but he has left it till the following day. He departs and we have not established whether he was the host's younger brother, the young Girl's fiancé, a commissioner of police, a pastor, or the co-creator of the design of the middle span of the great bridge. He has left—and what is stranger (!) in a theatrical show—he never returns. He doesn't appear on the stage during this performance, which lasts (according to my intentions) from thirty to seventy minutes. Even the avant-garde theater did not have such things. And yet they do occur in my realistic theater, my poetic theater. I warn any possible simple-minded producers of this play that he is not a symbolical character or a ghost or a dream vision. For this gentleman had already exchanged a few words with the* WOMAN *behind the door. Alas, these words reached neither us nor the (perhaps) intrigued audience. As a realist I do not recognize any theatrical, film, or novel "time." My time is identical with the time mirrored by our watches. The "dramatic" incidents which I have so far described last, let's say, three minutes. My wish is that the potential producers should extend these events to last ten minutes. But I do appreciate that in our times such dreams are futile. Theaters and producers (not to mention the public) will not stand for such consistent and brutal stage realism. In these circumstances, having sketched the likely course of the development of my theater, I once more disclaim all responsibility, I reach a compromise and proceed to build a spectacle based on elements of a traditional pseudo-avant-*

8

garde theater, but at certain points I shall realize the assumptions of my true theater about which I have spoken in these stage directions. In principle, a part of the spectacle has already been put into effect in accordance with these assumptions—I will nevertheless repeat once more the first scene in the compromise version.

SCENE ONE

A large room in the apartment of a distinguished CIVIL ENGINEER. *It's midnight. The clock on the wall strikes twelve. When the last stroke sounds a very beautiful, shapely* GIRL *enters through the door leading to the left. She is carrying a large leather suitcase. The room also contains a door which leads to the right and a door in the center. Passing by the table the* GIRL *trips against a chair. She drops the suitcase on the floor. She sits at the table and holds her head in her hands. A moment later she goes to the door on the left and presses her face against its white varnished surface. She is motionless and speechless. Then she returns to the table with a swift, decisive movement. Her hands are stretched down by her sides. Her palms slowly clench themselves into fists. There is a silver sugar bowl on the table. The lumps of sugar glisten in the electric light. There is something eerie in this landscape. Something clean and cruel at the same time. A black fly sleeps on one of the lumps of sugar. At a certain moment the fly takes off in a droning heavy flight. If it were possible to make use of a real fly in this scene that would have a considerable significance for the development of the action. Alas, limited resources do not permit such experiments on the large stages of contemporary professional theaters, although I did see elephants in a certain opera and horses in a certain play; another had dogs, cats, etc. . . . Because of these difficulties I decide against introducing a fly onto the stage. I had forgotten to add that the action of our play takes place in one of the neutral rich smallish capitalist countries where the percentage of suicides is higher than in economically underdeveloped countries. Psychological and mental diseases also have a richer harvest there than in other countries. Of course you can base the action in any country you can think*

11

of. In that case, however, you would have to alter certain props, such as furniture, doors, chairs, and so on. The GIRL *has started up from the table. And yet the calmness with which she uttered her first words seems to have immobilized and paralyzed her. Her lips opened with difficulty, as if somebody were prizing them open with a metal tool from outside. In an animal grimace she bared white, almost cruel (in this empty room) teeth. Although I appreciate at this moment the risk (I may simply become the laughingstock of our poor theater critics) of an unduly detailed description of the Girl's teeth I will do it, giving way to the dictates of my theater. The* GIRL *has two fillings, they are however fixed so discreetly and adroitly that a member of the audience could see them only with the help of glasses (not opera glasses but field glasses employed by the military and by explorers). Please forgive me the little joke on the subject of glasses. This allows me to catch my breath. I put off the decisive moment but of course I know the* GIRL *must speak. Although at the moment I have an inclination to remove her from the stage, she ought to pass across it without a word. But I lack the courage and the logic. Let's therefore begin the show.*

GIRL: They *(pause)*
    they there
    (louder) they there together

Silence. She stops her mouth with her hands as though with a gag. She takes her hands away slowly, very slowly. In the light her lips appear swollen, bloodshot, they move like suckers of parasites. She speaks softly but clearly.

They are doing
they are doing that there

Silence. She closes her eyes. She speaks with her eyes closed.

how long
how disgustingly long

12

how long are they doing it
how revoltingly
how long
they will never finish
they will never stop
twice three times five ten twelve

She runs to the door, raises both her hands, stands thus for a while, returns, sits at the table, buries her head in her arms.

after all I am a living being
I hear feel see
through that door
I am not a chair
animals
filthy animals
frogs apes dogs rabbits tortoises
how long can one go on doing this
one hour two three four

Silence.

they've stopped

Silence. She is listening.

they've stopped

She breathes.

O God what
they

She listens.

they are starting
how can they
they don't take any notice of anyone
like dogs
beneath the statue of Bismarck or Columbus

in a square under the gaze of children
under the gaze

*The Girl's body grows taut and stiff, she falls on the floor
and turns into a trembling bundle of hair and rags.*

stop

Whispering.

I beg you stop
I
I wished
I beg you

She crawls toward the door on her knees. Suddenly she begins to strike with her fingers at the silent white door, rhythmically at long intervals. She talks to herself.

I am mad
how can I
how can I behave like that
they are adults
it's I who am disgusting

Listens.

they are starting again
my head's splitting
how it creaks
how cruelly it creaks
how it cracks
my poor head
as though in a forest
or a sawmill
what the hell
are they sawing that divan with a fret saw

*She sits at the table; now under control, she talks smilingly
to herself, to the potential audience.*

14

Scene One

joke after all it's a joke coke smoke broke stroke trough
tough torture vulture vault malt fault lout loot love lust
life lifeblood strife rife wife wed wedded wedlock

At this point she speaks seriously, harshly.

random ripple rubbish rubble rupture reddish rhinoceros
rescue rest roll rush rich rough rack hack hack saw saw
with a knife with a saw

*She falls silent. Listens. Silence. Silence reigns in the room,
silence behind the closed door. An absolute and intolerable
silence. The girl writes something on a pink card and slides
it under the sugar bowl.*

how quiet
how quiet it is here
how quiet it is there why is it so quiet there
why don't they speak why aren't they talking
no cries no laughter no moans no groans
why do they

She gets up from the table and walks on tiptoe.

breathe
what are they doing there

She speaks softly.

I beseech you speak
laugh
say something
do you hear say something!
dumb animals
damned reptiles amphibians crustaceans protozoans
slipperworts

The GIRL *runs to the door and begins to batter it with her
fists.*

Speak! Speak!

She utters wild cries. She picks up her suitcase and runs out of the room through the center doorway.

SCENE TWO

The clock strikes the hour. An elderly but robust and healthy WOMAN *enters through the door on the left. Her complexion betrays a country origin. In fact the* WOMAN *was born and spent her childhood in a mountain village in an area where even today wolves may be seen. Let me stress once more, she is no doddery old girl. She is wearing a simple nightgown and her shoulders are covered with a warm woolen shawl. For twenty years now the* WOMAN *has been the Engineer's* HOUSEKEEPER. *After his wife died, for a while she breast-fed the poor orphan, the daughter who a moment ago left forever for North America. The "HOUSE-KEEPER" ought really to "burst" into the room with a cry of "God, what is happening here!" Alas, she is too late. In any case, she sleeps soundly, and did not hear the Girl's cries. Although it is now an hour since anything happened in this room, let's allow the* WOMAN *to utter this traditional, well-tried exclamation. Only in this way will we be able to convey the terror and turmoil which perturb this simple yet still-energetic person.*

ROBUST WOMAN *(Enters the empty silent room. She looks around and as though she had suddenly remembered something she utters a "soft cry")*: God, what's happening here! *(Since, however, nothing is happening she goes to the table, puts her hand in the sugar bowl, and places a lump of sugar in her mouth. First one lump, then, after a pause—lasting about three seconds—a second one, then a third and fourth . . .*

16

Altogether she might put five to six lumps in her mouth. When she is about to put in the fifth lump she notices the letter lying under the sugar bowl. The lumps of sugar deform the woman's cheeks and lips. Because this simple country woman is not terribly literate and reads very slowly, the scene with the letter may even be a very long one. In this way my play begins to stretch into a full-scale spectacle (not bad, eh?) and may be played upon even the biggest stages of the established theaters. I must confess I can't—sufficiently—"marvel" at our contemporary producers and directors who demand plays which are long; that is—as they say—"full-length." This demands a huge volume of words. Dialogue. Verbiage. Witticisms. Proverbs. Whereas drama takes place in silence. In an ocean of silence. And words are only tiny (coral) islands scattered in this infinite space. The already dated theater of Dürrenmatt, Frisch, and even Witkiewicz resembles a textbook rewritten in dialogue form. It has very little in common with the realistico-poetic theater. With the theater which I now wish to present to our producers and critics. But the trouble is that I too am not without guilt, although . . . the alert member of the audience will here notice that the door is opening . . .) What's that? *(The* WOMAN *slowly opens her mouth. One or at most two lumps of sugar may drop out of it onto the table or the floor.)* What is this? *(She reads the letter attentively once more and sits down on the chair.)* Well, just imagine! *(She wrings her hands.)* The Mistress . . . Holy Michael Archangel! *(Michael the Archangel, the holy prince and leader of the choir of angels, withstood Lucifer and the rebellious angels and with the cry "Mi-ka-el!" = "Who like God!," led the hosts faithful to God to a victorious battle (Revelation 12). Revered as the protector of the Church, the defender in the fight with Satan, the conductor of souls in their last journey to eternity, in the East also a patron of the sick. The Western Church celebrates two feasts in his honor: the chief one, on September 29, being the anniversary of the dedication of the Church of St. Michael and All Angels at via Salaria in Rome in the sixth century, and the second one on May 8 in memory of the Archangel's appearance on the Gargano Hill in Italy, also in the sixth century—according to the Encyclopedia of Saints, by Bishop K. Rodonski, in the St. Wojciech Library.)* Holy Michael Archangel! What does this mean? *(Puts on her glasses and reads.)* "Daddy, I can't bear this any longer, I am leaving forever, don't try looking for me. I shall never stop loving you. You must understand. I am no longer a child. I don't condemn you. You do what everybody does. I weep as I write these words. No, I am not crying any longer, I am smiling at you. Bye-bye. Your little daughter." *(The* WOMAN *goes to the half-open door and looks for a while into the dark empty hall.)* It had to end like that. *(She sits on the chair with her arms along her sides. She is holding the letter in her left hand.)* What's to be done now?

Yes, quite! In an "avant-garde" play the ENGINEER *would have "burst" upon the stage (through the other door) in his dressing gown and with his leg in a plaster cast, his nightshirt unbuttoned (at the chest). His chest is covered with black hair. Following him, the trembling* NURSE *in a diaphanous nylon smock (reaching down only to the middle of her thighs) and in a white cap with a black ribbon. Trembling and yet already feeling herself the mistress of the house. Now the* HOUSEKEEPER *hands the letter to the* ENGINEER, *who of course makes use of the telephone. He will at once inform the Chief Statistical Office. In five minutes' time the* COMMISSIONER *would have arrived. There would follow conversations, dialogues, telephone calls, and so on. For example:*

ENGINEER: It's your duty, Commissioner, to return my daughter.
COMMISSIONER: We shall do everything in our power. *(Dials.)*

ENGINEER: Surely she hasn't already flown to North America?
COMMISSIONER: Please be calm.

Looks through an international flights timetable. Meanwhile the ENGINEER *is pouring out brandies.*

Yes, since November 24, on Tuesdays, Fridays, and Saturdays there is a Boeing 707 flight from Frankfurt to New York via London.

ENGINEER: When does the plane leave Frankfurt?
COMMISSIONER: At 15:45.
ENGINEER: Landing in New York?
COMMISSIONER: At 19:30 local time.
ENGINEER: And what is the difference between our time and theirs?
COMMISSIONER: I'm sorry, I don't know.
ENGINEER: So at this moment the plane is already landing in New York?
COMMISSIONER: Yes, but please be calm.

They are drinking brandy. In the "surrealist" theater the Archangel Michael leading a host of angels would have descended from heaven in response to the Housekeeper's call, wearing gilt armor and brandishing a fiery sword. With this sword he strikes the white door of the Engineer's study. The door opens slowly. A frail girl dressed as a nurse is pushing a chromium-plated serving cart. The ENGINEER *is sitting on it. His left leg, in plaster, is stretched out, and as though on display. This leg, measuring about two meters, appears rather like some antediluvian monster. It makes a big impression on everyone. The* HOUSEKEEPER—*who had earlier been the wet nurse and (perhaps) the Engineer's mistress—covers her eyes with her hand. The* NURSE *pushes the cart toward the* HOUSE-KEEPER. *The* ENGINEER *grips the* HOUSEKEEPER *by the throat.*

ENGINEER: You dirty nigger.

The WOMAN *speaks in Swahili.*

Where is my child?

The WOMAN *replies in Swahili.*

So here I was not getting enough sleep during the past ten years in order to construct the bridge, while you couldn't even look after my girl.

WOMAN *(in a gruff voice):* She has run away to North America.

The ENGINEER *strangles the erstwhile black wet nurse. Angelic choirs conducted by Michael the Archangel are singing sixteenth-century motets.*

My imagination had run amuck (the soul straining for Paradise?). But let's return to reality. To our performance. The ROBUST WOMAN *wakes as though from a sleep.*

ROBUST WOMAN: And what are they doing over there? *(She glances "knowingly" in the direction of the Engineer's study. Shrugs her shoulders—just as in "life.")* What can they be doing there? Nothing. They are sleeping. *(She talks to herself.)* You have a hundred kilos of plaster on your left leg!

NOTE: I have been caught in my own booby trap. When I sat down to write this play I was in an excellent humor. I must confess that when writing the stage directions I was amusing myself. What was the source of that carefree optimism? Simply that together with the whole of humanity I took a deep breath. The apocalypse veiled its countenance. For some time now the world has seemed to me a more durable and more solid construction. I will not conceal the fact that the change of my mood has been influenced by a political act of significance for humanity as a whole. I am thinking of the nuclear test ban. Despite stupid gossip I am a man who likes to have a laugh; as for the fact that I had never laughed in a cemetery! . . . So I started writing this comedy in a cheerful mood. It seems to me that there is an atmosphere favoring the rejuvenation of the theater, of the theater as a game. I admit that in my previous plays I had tried to create just such a new theater. I failed. Breathing apocalypse, I could not entertain others (and entertain myself). Thus my plays were not quite accurate realizations of my intentions. At a certain moment they would turn into the so-called "true theater." But where does the continuation of the "true theater" lead? To such monstrous works as The Physicists, Andorra, *and many plays by American, Crakow, French, Warsaw, Austrian (and other) playwrights. Dialogues on the subjects of politics, sociology, religion, and sex, lasting for several hours and fitted into traditional "dramatic" peripateia of the "Heroes," have simply become a nightmare. The writers try to astonish the public, shake it, amuse it, and at the same time they write in dialogue form naïve stories which have occurred in the family of some solicitor, industrialist, scientist, and so on. B—— is quite close to the theater in the "spirit" of entertainment . . . yet theater critics have turned him into a mystic, a nihilist. A tragedian. Whereas his plays are wonderful entertainment. They ought to be performed in music halls and student theaters. But to understand this, one has to be an optimist. This Shakespeare of our times (despite the fact that he has written only three or four plays) is being interpreted so one-sidedly that he will eventually cease to be readable and acceptable. This is the fault of producers and critics. Surely* Waiting for Godot *may be interpreted as an excellent comedy. But to do that, one really has to be a realist, a person of serious intent who "is not waiting for Godot." As it is, the metaphysical beagles have smelled carrion for themselves and are indulging in mysticism, they terrify dumb common people (who believe for example in Michael the Archangel, Lucifer, and so on). This reciprocal mystification which is played at by stage designers, directors, critics, and the public leads to . . . a dark room in which the*

21

*children frighten themselves with ghosts. Unfortunately, the
children are now grown up and the whole show is changing
into a lurid ritual. (NB: I am aware that I am at this moment
stretching B—— too much in support of my thesis but at a
time when I propose a completely new interpretation of his
plays I can't avoid extremes and overemphasis.) This same
mystification appears in relation to other plays by B——.
Instead of enjoying themselves at his* Endgame *people are
searching for lousy nihilism. Surely a right-thinking person
will not accuse one who is grown-up, wise, and indeed a
dramatist (almost) of genius of treating the "theater" seriously when he places the aged parents in ashcans. The same
applies to another play where the "heroes" are buried in
sand. The action should of course be set in a large sandpit
among children who are building sand castles, throwing sand
at each other and, when necessary, peeing into the sand. As
it is, all this is placed in some metaphysical sand and a ma-
cabre (and of course a quite senseless) spectacle is mounted.
So one can't be surprised that the* Frankfurter Allgemeine
*reviewer writes nonsense on the subject of the world première
of B——'s latest play which took place in Ulm. "Classical"
plays (from the Greeks right up to Dürrenmatt) have so re-
stricted the horizons of our reviewers that they treat all plays
(the contemporary ones too) "seriously." A theater which
never had anything in common with so-called "real life" became the field of the strangest and most entertaining misunderstanding. Had this "spiritually" impoverished reviewer
of the* Frankfurter Allgemeine *eventually understood that the
theater is not a dramatized reflection of "real life," he would
not have been ironic (causing amusement among the uniniti-
ated) on the subject of live corpses "buried up to their necks
in something or other." These same people who easily swal-
low* A Midsummer Night's Dream, Balladyna *(Slowacki's),
Goldoni, Ibsen . . . these same people suddenly become impoverished realists and deride the poet-dramatist who dared*

Scene Two

*to place people in ashcans, in the ground, or in urns. They
raised no objections to people being placed in hell or in
heaven but they can't come to terms with people who entertain themselves with conversation on a rubbish heap. This is
strange indeed! After this brief explanation which will perhaps give you a clearer idea of my theater I return to the interrupted dramatic action.*

ROBUST WOMAN *(talking to herself):* Enough of this game, my
doves.

That old tomcat! Just look at him. His leg's in plaster
weighing a ton I shouldn't be surprised and all he can think
of is dalliance. And what can they be doing over there? In
such a position. *(Takes a book from the shelf, skims through
it, reads not very audibly.)*

Carezza or coitus reservatus . . . mmm . . . hmmm . . .
mmm . . . well . . . standard position . . . mmmm . . . *(Mumbles.)* Ah well, yes! soixante-neuf . . . or as we would say,
sixty-nine . . . the things people think up . . . twenty-one . . .
*(Replaces the book on the shelf, dries her hands against her
blouse in a peasant manner as if she had a moment before
been feeding the poultry or blowing the children's noses.)*

My young mistress, my poor child is gone to North
America without a coat. She hasn't put on anything warm.
That rain! That rain! Won't it ever stop? And just before
her finals. She packed, and ciao! All the same, the old one
could also have arranged things differently! Ah well, if it's
got to be "bye-bye" then it's "bye-bye." *(Goes to the door.
Listens. After a moment, knocks gently.)* Nobody answers.
They must be asleep. And that little viper has twisted the
Master round her finger. A nurse. Well, and couldn't even an
old one like me pull it and even set it? . . . There came the
little thing in its cap and clutching a bag. Such a little wet
hen. Only had one lump of sugar in her tea. And then, just
watch that little hen! Just my luck. The old tom. He snatched

23

the hen onto a spit and crunched her up but she too knows
what's what. Oh God, God. In one's old age one can't even
remember whether one says "crunched" with a "c" or a "k."
The old head is in a terrible spin.

The clock on the wall strikes the hour. The WOMAN *sits at
the table. From a little bag in her bosom she pulls out a little
notebook bound in stiff green covers. She opens the notebook
and begins to write. She talks aloud as though she were dic-
tating to herself . . .*

"The night from September 6 to 7, 1963.

"An hour ago the Mistress left the house forever, departing for North America. She has left a farewell letter
under the sugar bowl. The master is still locked up with his
nurse in his study. For the past twenty-four hours they have
not been partaking of any nourishment. At first I condemned
him but I don't think I was right. The late Mistress was a
true Viridiana: ice, marble, and wood. Often enough the
Master would return straight from the bridge and the water
cold and shivering, and she wouldn't cuddle him. Cold. A
wretched frigid soul. Last week they cemented the last pillar
in the cofferdam. What's to be done? But one can't be surprised at the young Mistress. I ought to leave domestic serv-
ice and set up a poultry farm. I have been dreaming of this
for the past twenty years, although the state of the market at
the moment is not too good. We don't know the outcome of
the Brussels negotiations regarding the reduction of tariffs on
chickens imported from North America. The raising of tariffs
on European products would have been a severe blow for
France, Italy, West Germany, and other countries of the
Common Market. Tariff on cheeses would have risen from
twelve per cent of their price to thirty-five per cent. But what
are we to do with our chicken and eggs! Only ten years ago
a French or an Italian chicken would lay on average eighty

24

eggs a year, now poultry batteries produce on average 220 to 250 eggs a year." (WOMAN *stops writing and thinks. There is no sound behind the door of the Engineer's study.*) I'll go to bed . . . *(Stretches and yawns.)* I feel hungry . . . Omne vivum ex ovo. *(She goes to the cupboard, takes out a mug, two eggs, a saucer and a small spoon. She breaks the eggs, at the same time skillfully separating the yolks from the whites. She slips the yolks into the mug which has a little red rose painted on it. Beating the eggs into a gogel-mogel, she sings softly.)*

Two eggs	Two
will I beat	will I
for you	two for you
my child	my bonny
my bonny	my child
child	a sweet
a sweet	just for you
gogel-mogel	my child
just for you	for you
my child	will I beat
my bonny	gogel-mogel
child	for you

The WOMAN *is beating the yolks in the mug. How long? As long as it is necessary to beat the eggs. This may last five minutes and, with intervals, even twelve. Here again is a place where the (potential) producer may intervene. Depending on the size of the stage and on the managing director, one can either shorten or lengthen the egg-beating scene, although within the limits set by the author. All exaggeration in either direction would push the spectacle down to the level of a farce—which at present is the stand-by of all impotents in the theater.*

SCENE THREE

The same room. The door to the right and the door to the left are closed. The middle door leading to the hall is ajar. There is no sugar bowl on the table. Evidently it has been put away by the ROBUST WOMAN. *Nor can we see the flies which were to appear in previous scenes. Although at the moment the stage is empty, tension rises continuously. The situation is tense. It seems that something ought to happen. The closed door leading to the Engineer's study gradually changes its shape. It seems to acquire larger proportions, it expands to achieve (perhaps) a symbolic role. All this is of course happening exclusively in the spectator's imagination. In reality the door remains as it is.*

Before I start writing this scene I wish to share (with those interested) the thoughts that accompanied me while I was planning it. I am here introducing the STRANGER *(who is not connected, in the "dramatic sense," with any of the characters who appear in this play). This man lives in a very similar street, in a very similar house, and in an almost identical apartment to that of the* ENGINEER. *Both houses have been built by the same firm. The apartments possess identical furniture, carpets, pictures. The people who live in these apartments read the same magazines and books. At the same time they watch the same TV programs, listen to the same speeches, sermons, and concerts of light and serious music. They have very similar fashionable clothes and information because they have been to similar schools and universities. On their walls they have almost identical pictures. Their refrigerators are stocked with identical food products, e.g., frozen chickens, bananas, sausages, and so on. With similar interiors they live similar lives. They have similar pleasures, problems, deviations, illnesses, and children. They have an identical vocabulary of words, expressions, sayings, jokes, curses, and so on. They have a similar pattern of life and death. They differ in their surnames but often their Christian names are identical. Their reminiscences from the past and plans for the future are almost identical. It is the same with their shirts and their cars. The same doctors tell them the same things at the same time and so do politicians and priests. They spend their vacations in the same resorts, look at the same landscapes, castles, and archeological sights. Only their faces (partly) and fingerprints prove that they are not the same people. We shouldn't be surprised that the man who entered the Engineer's apartment feels quite at home. Almost throughout the whole scene he doesn't realize that he is in somebody else's apartment. So, contrary to appearance, our drama develops consistently, and this is my constant concern. As we know, the "stranger" has played a large role in various old and new plays. But in the development of the usually naïve (dramatic, God help us) action this "stranger" suddenly turns out to be the father lost in the war, the prodigal son, the uncle who has come back from Africa (or America), a school friend, a suicide who has been cut off or fished out and is restored to life, an insurance agent, a thief, and so on and so on. Worthy classical and avant-garde (!) playwrights make very skillful use of this "stranger" to surprise the audience, tangle the plot ... and unravel it toward the end. But my "stranger" has nothing at all to do with this drama I am presenting to you. He has found himself in the Engineer's apartment for the reasons I have already exhaustively explained. A similar street, a similar house, a similar door, similarly painted walls, identical furniture, tapestries, carpets, pictures . . . even the brandy in the cabinet bears the same label. Similar glasses. He could have made a mistake. Of course. And he wasn't drunk (that would have been too easy), oh no! Writing, or rather writing the dialogue for the third scene of this play, I was quite aware that this is material for a great, truly contemporary comedy. After all, it could have*

*happened that "the wife" is so little different from "the wife,"
"the daughter" from "the daughter," a "conversation" from a
"conversation," "love" from "love," that right to the end our
"hero" would not realize that he has got the apartments mixed
up. Perhaps one day I shall make use of this idea and in this connection I request sundry speculators not to try to . . . they know
what.*

*Following this "intrusion" we return to the room and to the play.
A man who will be forty-two in three days' time enters the room.
We cannot, alas, show this to the audience (from the stage). He is
wearing a fashionably cut coat (I don't indeed know what cut is
fashionable but the producer or the stage designer can look this
up in a slick). It's a black coat, maybe even a jacket of thick
fashionable (?) material. The coat is unbuttoned, apparently the
man is in a state of excitement. He has no hat and his hair is
damp (of course this fact is of no consequence). The STRANGER
has entered the room warily but not on tiptoe. It looks as though
he were trying to surprise someone (but not quite). Rather, he is
undecided. He sits at the table, lights a cigarette, looks at a
"fixed point." He sees "nothing" around him. His formal suit (it
may be a dinner jacket) demonstrates that the man has returned
from an official reception at an embassy or from a concert (maybe
he is the conductor). It pains me to write about a certain small
detail but unfortunately I am forced to do this by the poetics of
this drama: well, this (almost) elegant gentleman has a hole in his
left sock. This is a remnant of very ancient times when women
darned socks and Ibsen was worshiped. I can't, alas, explain how
this sock with a hole found itself on the foot of a well-situated conductor or bank manager. Of course the hole in the sock is tiny
and is (definitely!) invisible: it is hidden away in the patent-
leather shoe. "If this hole is not visible, why do you write so
much about it?" a simple-minded member of the audience or a
crafty drama theorist might ask. Quite so. In this play I write not
only about the visible world but also about the invisible (real)*

*world. But our producers of course demand that we should occupy
ourselves with holes in heaven (because a hole in the sock is too
small for the large stage of the national theater). Hold it, gentlemen! Sometimes a tiny little hole may be more dramatic than a
hole in heaven. I personally do not ignore even a hole in cheese.
True, "a hole in heaven" opens possibilities for stage designers,
composers, reviewers, and so on and so on. Stage settings for "a
hole in heaven" are quite a spectacle, a self-sufficient spectacle!
But here? It's a flop. Our ways part, gentlemen. You see a huge
stage with a huge hole in heaven, while I am satisfied with a hole
in a sock. Again, I am rambling on, while "nothing is happening
on the stage" (a fact which is an underrated asset of the poetic
theater—apparently nothing, and yet everything . . .). The man
is still smoking a cigarette. He goes to the cabinet, pulls out a bottle of brandy and a glass. He pours. He looks around.*

SCENE FOUR

The same room in the Engineer's apartment. The STRANGER *has
apparently realized that he had entered someone else's apartment
and has gone. He has left behind an empty brandy bottle and a
glass. A man in a rubber raincoat and rubber boots reaching
above the knees bursts "like a bomb" (this superb simile is however very difficult to put into effect) into the room. He looks as
though he has been fished out of the water. He is dripping. To the
extent that in the spot where he has stopped, a large pool of
water is forming on the parquet floor under our very eyes. He is
the* FIRST DEPUTY *of the* CHIEF ENGINEER. *He is followed by two
well-built handsome* WORKERS *in boiler suits. Their pockets are
bulging with spanners, spirit measures, set squares, micrometers,
and other instruments indispensable in building large-scale
edifices.*

FIRST DEPUTY *(looks around confused. The door to the left and the door to the right are both closed):* Is anybody there? *(Silence.)* Hey, is anybody there? *(Silence.)* What does this mean? The water has broken through the embankment and has washed away the dike, the dam, the lock and even the island! It's rising every minute. Any moment now it will flood the boulevards and the whole town! Hey, is there anyone there?

Sound of a cannon shot. This is the flood alarm. A moment following the shot the ROBUST WOMAN *holding a candle in her trembling hand enters the room.*

ROBUST WOMAN: Was it you who knocked?

FIRST DEPUTY: Yes.

ROBUST WOMAN: At last! I have been waiting these three days. Please follow me.

They all disappear in the open doorway but the ensuing dialogue is clearly audible.

Everything's blocked up. The shower. The faucet, the tank, the window, the drainpipe, the sink, the toilet, the bidet, the thermometer, the children's tub, the toothpaste . . . they throw hair everywhere . . . fluff all over the place.

FIRST DEPUTY: Where is the Engineer?

ROBUST WOMAN: What do you want the Engineer for? He is asleep.

FIRST DEPUTY: Don't you understand, woman, that the steel ropes of the suspension bridge that was dedicated last week may snap at any moment? The balustrade is twisted, the tower is leaning over, water is already lapping against the bridgehead.

ROBUST WOMAN: Against the icebreaker.

FIRST DEPUTY: The icebreaker, the icebreaker! Both the pillar and the central span are caving in.

ROBUST WOMAN: What pillar? In a suspension bridge?

FIRST DEPUTY: Where is the Engineer?

Scene Four

ROBUST WOMAN: He is in bed with his leg in plaster.
FIRST DEPUTY: Then wake him up!
ROBUST WOMAN *(shrugging her shoulders)*: Well?

FIRST DEPUTY *taps delicately on the door.* ROBUST WOMAN *looks at the empty brandy bottle and sniffs the glass. There is silence behind the door.*

FIRST DEPUTY: Hey, hey, Chief!

Pause.

I am very sorry
but the pillar of the middle span is caving in
Chief, please get up
we must drive at once
to the place
of the imminent disaster

Silence.

FIRST WORKER *(with a crafty look)*: I smell a rat.
ROBUST WOMAN: And what are you up to?
FIRST WORKER: If they hadn't sanded the cement, the pillar wouldn't have given way.
FIRST DEPUTY: Go toward the bridge. For the time being secure the icebreaker with sandbags. I will try to wake the Engineer.

WORKERS *leave.* FIRST DEPUTY *bangs on the closed door with his fists.*

Chief, Chief
I implore you
in the name of our old friendship
from our schooldays
will you please come with me at once
don't you remember our old history teacher
or our biology teacher
with his tinted beard! Was it green or

31

ginger—I can't quite remember . . .
We used to call him alga . . . protozoan . . .
slipperwort . . .

ROBUST WOMAN *nods her head indulgently and leaves the room.*

Open up! You lazybones!

DEPUTY *strikes the door with his fist. Silence behind the closed door.* DEPUTY *runs and hits the door with the whole weight of his body. Like a battering ram. Once, twice, three times . . .*

THE CARD INDEX

••

I am not offering a list of characters. The play's "hero" is of indeterminate age, occupation, and appearance. On various occasions our "hero" ceases to be the hero of our tale and is replaced by other "heroes." Many of those who take part in this chronicle do not have significant roles, while others, who might have played the lead, are often not allowed to express themselves or have little to say. The place of the action doesn't change. The stage setting doesn't change. A chair moved once during the whole performance will be enough. And the time . . .

The play is realistic and takes place in the present. The chair is real, all the objects and pieces of furniture are real. Their measurements are slightly larger than normal. An ordinary average room.

Table. Bookcase. Two chairs. A sink. A bed on high legs. The room has no windows. There are doors at the opposite ends. Both doors remain open all the time. The bed stands against the wall. The light in the room, ordinary daylight, remains constant throughout. The lights are not switched off even when the tale is ended. The curtain doesn't fall. Perhaps the tale is only interrupted. For an hour, for a year . . .

One further remark. People appear in their ordinary everyday clothes. They mustn't be dressed up in any striking apparel, gaudy rags, or other similar accessories. The stage design is of no consequence. The fewer stage effects the better.

Various people pass through the doors: some move quickly, others slowly. From time to time we hear snatches of conversation. Some stop to read a newspaper. It appears as though there is a street passing through the Hero's room. Some stop to eavesdrop on the conversation in the Hero's room. They may add a few words and then move on. The action is continuous throughout.

HERO *(lying on the bed, his arms supporting the back of his head. He stretches out one hand and holds it up to his face):* This is my hand. I am moving my hand. My hand. *(Moving his fingers.)* My fingers. My hand is so obedient. It does everything I tell it to.

Turns toward the wall. Falls asleep perhaps. The Hero's parents enter. They look worried. FATHER *glances at his watch.*

MOTHER: Don't keep your hands under the bedclothes. It isn't nice and it isn't healthy.

FATHER: What will become of him if he lies around in bed like this? Up you get, my boy!

MOTHER: At forty he's only a music-hall manager!

FATHER: He's playing a nasty game under those bedclothes. I'm sure of it. All by himself.

MOTHER: Nonsense! Can't you see there's someone else under there? I think it's a woman.

FATHER: You're mad! A seven-year-old boy . . . Pinched a quarter from me yesterday . . . I'll beat him for that! And he scrounges sugar from the sugar bowl.

MOTHER: But he's due at a board meeting, with speeches for and against.

FATHER: He stole a quarter from me. If he'd only said, "Daddy, please give me a quarter. I want to buy something," I would have given him one. He must be punished!

MOTHER: Quiet! He's asleep.

FATHER: Who does he take after?

Enter CHORUS OF ELDERS. *There are three of them. Dressed in creased, rather shabby suits. One is wearing a hat. They sit by the wall in folding chairs they bring with them. They move about despondently but recite their scripts very clearly in ringing tones and without undue mimicry. The* CHORUS OF

ELDERS *takes advantage of breaks in the action; it imparts lessons, issues warnings, creates confidence.*

CHORUS OF ELDERS:

He who in childhood cut off Hydra's head,
Will in his youth the blood of Centaurs shed,
Will rescue victims of the Demon,
Will gather laurels up in Heaven.*

FATHER *(leaning over the bed, takes the Hero's ear between two fingers and pulls it):* Don't pretend you're asleep. Get up when your father is talking to you.

HERO: Stop! Stop! Who goes there? Stop, or I'll shoot! Halt!

MOTHER: He's talking in his sleep. Ah, that terrible war.

FATHER: I want to talk to you, you little monkey.

HERO *(sitting up in bed):* I'm listening.

FATHER: Why did you eat all the sugar in the sugar bowl?

HERO: That was Bolek.

FATHER: Don't tell lies, tell me exactly how it was.

HERO: Something tempted me, Daddy, some devil, Daddy . . .

FATHER: If you had said: "Daddy, may I have some sugar . . ."

HERO: But, Daddy, you were picking your nose. I spied on you . . .

FATHER: Viper! What will you grow up into? God is my witness . . .

MOTHER: How dare you talk to your father like that . . . I don't recognize you, my child.

FEMALE VOICE UNDER THE BEDCLOTHES: It's time for the meeting, sir.

HERO: Mom and Dad, after thirty years I have realized the enormity of my sins. Yes, it was I who ate the sausage on Good Friday, the fifteenth of April, 1926. I am ashamed of my act. Olek and Teofilek and I schemed for days to eat

---

* This is a quotation from a famous Polish classic, "Ode to Youth," by Adam Mickiewicz.—*Tr.*

that sausage. My dastardly act, dearest Dad, can't be excused. I ate the sausage out of greed. I wasn't hungry. Thanks to your care, Dad, I had enough bread in my childhood. I also had pocket money for sweets. Nevertheless, I erred.

MOTHER: But your father is asking you about the sugar, not the sausage.

HERO: Mom, don't defend me. Renounce your son. I ate both the sugar and the sausage. I remember that we began eating the sausage at about 15.05 hours. I had the biggest share. I also planned the removal of our dearest granny.

MOTHER: But Granny died a natural death . . .

HERO: My poor parents! You've spawned a monster. For ten years I had, with malice aforethought, been adding strychnine to Granny's sponge cake. I also well remember my despicable practices with matches. I now recollect with revulsion that I planned to remove Dad as well.

FATHER: This is a nice thing to hear!

HERO: These thoughts and plans were hatched in my head when I was five. I remember the five little candles that were glowing on the little birthday cake.

FEMALE VOICE UNDER THE BEDCLOTHES *(impatiently)*: It's time you went, sir.

HERO: I would also like to confess that . . .

FEMALE VOICE UNDER THE BEDCLOTHES: It really is time you went, sir.

HERO: As you can hear, a board meeting awaits me.

Parents leave.

FEMALE VOICE UNDER THE BEDCLOTHES: The meeting is not for another two hours, but you ought to be prepared. I will prepare you for everything.

CHORUS OF ELDERS:
Hush-a-bye, baby, on the tree top,
When the wind blows the cradle will rock;

When the bough breaks the cradle will fall,
Down will come baby, cradle, and all.

HERO *falls asleep. He is awakened by a gun explosion. The bang ought to be colossal, so as to frighten the audience as well!*

HERO: The idiots! War again?

FEMALE VOICE UNDER THE BEDCLOTHES: No sir, the Princess of Monaco has given birth to octuplets! In this connection follies and drolleries and such like are being organized throughout the country. From the peaks of the Tatra Mountains to the blue Baltic.

HERO: But why in Poland? The Princess resides in Monaco!

FEMALE VOICE UNDER THE BEDCLOTHES: This makes no difference. A hundred of our young activists will pay homage by traveling on motorscooters to the Congo. Others are making vows of chastity.

HERO *(looking at the ceiling)*: Buffoons. *(Pause.)* Idiots. *(Pause.)* Cretins, baboons, dungheaps, thieves, swindlers, pederasts, astronauts, onanists, sportsmen, feature writers, moralists, critics, bigamists. *(Pause. Lights a cigarette and looks at the ceiling.)* I am in bed. The chiefs of state and the chiefs of staff are allowing me to lie and look at the ceiling. The ceiling. The beautiful clean white ceiling. The bosses are so nice. I shall have a quiet Sunday.

OLGA *comes into the room. She is a middle-aged woman. She stops at the foot of the bed. Takes off her coat. Places her coat, bag, and scarf on the bed.*

OLGA: I was passing by and heard you calling me . . .

HERO: I calling you?

OLGA: It's fifteen years since you left home. You haven't given me a sign of life since.

HERO: That's true.

OLGA: You left no address.

HERO: I had none.

OLGA: You said you were going to get some cigarettes.

HERO: I got them.

OLGA: It's fifteen years since you went. How are you? Speak. Say something.

HERO: I'll tell you a joke.

OLGA: A joke at a moment like this? This is awful. He wants to tell me a joke after fifteen years . . .

HERO: I'd like a cup of tea.

OLGA: Tea, when I want an account of what you've been doing all this time! You've been a disappointment to me, Henryk.

HERO: My name is Victor.

OLGA: Victor, you've been a disappointment to me. You are a swine and a fraud.

HERO *(yawns):* I don't want to talk any more.

CHORUS OF ELDERS *(each* ELDER *talking to himself):* He doesn't want to talk . . . But he is the chief hero . . . Who else is there to talk?

OLGA *(stamping her foot at the* CHORUS*):* Shut up, you over there . . . If only you had said a word . . . But you didn't . . . Nothing!

HERO: I shall not achieve anything in these circumstances.

OLGA: You stroked my breasts, you fawned upon me like a snake, you seduced me with beautiful words.

HERO: Beautiful words?

OLGA: You said we would have a house with a garden, a couple of children, a son and a daughter . . . The world was coming to an end and you were lying! You broke . . .

HERO: The world didn't come to an end. We've come through. Oh, you can't imagine how glad I am to be lying down. I can lie down, trim my nails, listen to music. The bosses have given me the whole of Sunday. Why don't you come to bed? We'll talk.

OLGA: I musn't be late for the music show. I've already got my ticket . . . I will never forgive you. *(She leaves.)*

HERO: Leave me your newspaper. I thought we would all die, so I talked to you about children, flowers, life. It's quite simple. *(Opens the newspaper, looks through it, and reads aloud.)* "Before pouring beer into them, bottles ought to be carefully washed. The workers employed in this job often do not trouble themselves sufficiently to check whether the bottles are clean. The result is that, when filled, bottles appear to contain various foreign bodies. There are also cases of flies swimming in the beer. In our previous article on beer we wrote about the almost barbarous attitude toward this beverage on the part of the retail workers. The beer trade provides criminals with opportunities. For example, how can one turn a 100-liter barrel into a 120-liter barrel?"

CHORUS OF ELDERS: Very simply.

HERO: "All one has to do is to apply more froth to every glass of beer consumed. Instead of a full glass of beer, the customer receives a glass only half or a third full." *(His voice grows more powerful and tragic.)* "We agree that beer ought to possess the so-called head of froth, but we are concerned with the fact that the contents of a glass should relate to the norm. That is why all glasses ought to be marked showing where 250 or 500 cubic centimeters of drink come up to. Alas, the beer mugs are not even rinsed properly. The inside of the glass is covered with a film of grease, and grease is enemy number one of the golden drink. There is a culpable absence of responsibility in the beer trade. We must end this once and for all. We must punish . . ."

The CHORUS *splits up.*

FIRST ELDER *(putting his hand to his ear)*: What is he talking about?

SECOND ELDER: About beer!

THIRD ELDER: Does this beer contain allusions to the government, has it got hidden meanings, symbols, allegories, is our Hero an ideological watchdog?

40

FIRST ELDER: He is talking about beer.

SECOND ELDER: There must be something hidden in that beer!

THIRD ELDER: He says flies are swimming in the beer.

SECOND ELDER: Flies? Well, that's something.

FIRST ELDER: Rubbish! In his case beer means beer and a fly means a fly and nothing else.

THIRD ELDER: For heaven's sake, this is no hero. He is just a nonentity. Where are all the heroes of old, the bards, knights in armor, and the prophets? A fly in "small beer"! Not just beer, but small beer. What does it all mean?

SECOND ELDER *(twisting his face ironically):* It is the theater befitting our great age.

THIRD ELDER: The age appears great but the people are rather small.

FIRST ELDER: As always, as always.

THIRD ELDER: Flies swimming in small beer. There is something hidden in that.

> CHORUS *nods in agreement. There is dead silence, during which we hear the song of a canary. After a while, an old man with a mustache and an old hat enters the room.*

HERO: Uncle!

UNCLE: I've joined a pilgrimage to a monastery . . . I am calling on you on the way: "He descended into Hell, because it was on his way." And how are things with you, Frank?

HERO: So-so, so-so, Uncle. So many years. We haven't seen each other for twenty-five years, Uncle! *(Sits up on the bed and pulls up his socks.)* I'm sure your feet ache, Uncle. Must be a hundred kilometers. Do sit down, Uncle. How nice that you've called on me, Uncle. I'll prepare some water so you can soak your feet in it and I'll make some tea! Lie down, Uncle! Put your feet in the water. *(Pulls a washbasin from under the bed and pours water into it. He is pouring real water into a real basin from a real jug.)* Please, Uncle . . . In a minute I will . . . *(Overjoyed, he fusses around* UNCLE.*)*

Uncle, to uncle . . . of uncle . . . with uncle . . . oh uncle! . . . in uncle . . .

UNCLE: What a kind-hearted boy. Thank you, child, for this ceremonious welcome. *(Takes off his leggings and his socks. Soaks his feet in the basin.)* And how are things with you, Stefan?

HERO: Well, you see, Uncle, I was going to write to you, but Sophie said you were ill, so I thought you had died. *(Places his hands on Uncle's shoulders.)* I'm terribly glad to see you, Uncle. You have no idea, Uncle. How are things with you, Uncle?

UNCLE: Ah well, one has to push this barrow of life somehow. Nothing to get excited about.

HERO: But you are real, Uncle, and your hat is real. *(Takes Uncle's hat off.)* And your mustache is real, your feet are real, your trousers are real, your heart is real and your feelings and thoughts are real. A whole real uncle. Even your leggings are real, and the buttons, and your words. Real words! *(He is talking with mounting emotion and rapture.)*

UNCLE: Well, and how are you, Stefan? Helenka told me you've been to Paris.

HERO: Yes, I have.

UNCLE: Well, let's hear something about that Paris of yours. I will never get a chance to see it . . . Auntie is also curious.

HERO: With pleasure, Uncle.

UNCLE: Wasn't a waste of time, was it?

HERO: Of course not.

UNCLE: And how do people manage over there?

HERO: Oh, they manage somehow . . . *(Takes out his cigarettes.)* Would you like one? They're French.

UNCLE: If they are French, I'll take two.

HERO: I bought some matches in Paris, I bought toilet soap in Paris, a toothbrush, razor blades, shirts, perfumes, slippers, paper clips, pins, needles.

The CHORUS OF ELDERS *is examining some photographs. They laugh, tell each other stories; we can hear snatches of them.*

UNCLE: And what about the arts and literature? . . . And politics?

HERO: Well, it's so-so. You can't take it all in. You know something, Uncle, I've seen Napoleon, the Pope, the Queen, all life-size. All pink and made of wax. They eat a lot of salads, they eat cheese and drink wine. Of course the cooking is French.

UNCLE: So you've had a change of scene and you bought a thing or two.

HERO: You know, Uncle, this city lies in a bluish mist—like pure alcohol.

UNCLE *(after a pause):* But . . . well, you appear a little downcast. Oh, Romek, Romek, why do you worry so much?

HERO: Well, you see, Uncle . . . Ah, it's not worth talking about . . . I clapped. I cheered.

UNCLE: What do you mean "clapped"?

HERO: Just simply clapped.

UNCLE: Everybody clapped.

HERO: I am not interested in everybody. I am thinking of myself. I clapped.

UNCLE: You are a baby, Piotrysh. Picasso also clapped.

HERO: Oh, Uncle, Uncle . . .

UNCLE: What is it, then, Romek?

HERO: I know a lot of people clapped, but they have forgotten it by now. They now occupy themselves with the latest cars or enjoy themselves at masked balls, but I still put my hands together and that clapping still claps inside me. Sometimes there is such a colossal clapping in me. I am empty like a cathedral at night. Clapping, Uncle, clapping . . .

Silence.

UNCLE: Well, anyway, you are a miserable, weak, lifeless bunch. Bald and splitting hairs. What am I to say? All this clapping you people had to do is nothing in comparison. I remember during the disturbances we threw our commander into the tomato soup. Let's see, what was his name?

HERO: Into the soup?

UNCLE: It so happened there was some tomato soup bubbling in the cauldron. Times were uneasy. There were various incidents. Rebellions. In other words, things were boiling . . . He was making an inspection of the kitchen. Soup was being cooked for the whole company. We threw him in. We covered the cauldron with the lid and he got cooked together with his mustache. The spurs got cooked and the medals as well. Even now, I can't help laughing when I remember it. *(Pats HERO on the shoulders.)* You have a delicate conscience. I absolve you!

HERO: I am sad, Uncle. You know, Uncle, when I was a little boy, I played at being horses. I would turn into a horse and rush through the courtyard and the streets, my mane flying. But now, Uncle, I can't change into a human being though I am a director of an institute. I'd like to dig up the earth, pick out a potato or two and roast them for you, Uncle. Potatoes have a gray coarse skin. Inside they are white, soft, and hot. In my life, I would like to own an apple tree with little branches, leaves, blossoms, and apples . . . Such a long time since I've sat in the shade. Apples are covered with a transparent film of wax, fingerprints are clearly visible on such apples. Apples are hanging on branches. They are awaiting my hand. Just like girls.

UNCLE: Well, Romek, will you come home? We are all waiting for you: Mom and your sisters.

HERO: I can't, Uncle.

UNCLE: Don't you want to turn your back on the great big world?

HERO: No.

UNCLE: Haven't you eaten your fill?

HERO: My appetite is still growing, Uncle. Whenever I open my mouth I would gulp whole cities, people, buildings and paintings and breasts, TV sets, motors, stars, odalisques, socks, watches, titles, medals, pears, pills, newspapers, bananas, masterpieces.

UNCLE: Why not pack and come with me? Tomorrow you will be home.

HERO: No, Uncle, I can't go back.

UNCLE: Come, come, the birds are singing, spring's coming.

HERO: I have a lot of things to do, various matters to settle, I can't tear myself away from all this, I can't make head or tail of it. Later perhaps.

UNCLE *(dries his feet on the blanket, puts on his shoes, pushes the basinful of water under the bed):* Well, Henryk, I think I'll go now. God be with you.

He goes out. HERO *is silent. He lies with his eyes closed. Two men enter the room. One is wearing a cyclist's cap, the other a hat. They wear long, old-fashioned jackets. One of them draws some papers out of a briefcase; the other pulls out a metal measuring tape. They begin to measure the Hero's room. They do this with great meticulousness.*

MAN IN CAP: Three meters, forty-eight centimeters.

MAN IN HAT *writes.* MAN IN CAP *measures the door and the bed and calls out the figures.* MAN IN HAT *writes them down, adds, multiplies, and divides.* MAN IN CAP *comes over to the* HERO, *measures his length and breadth, his feet, the circumference of his head and neck, the width of his shoulders, etc.* MAN IN CAP *leans over* HERO.

What is he clutching in his hand?

MAN IN HAT: Papers.

MAN IN CAP: We will have to unclench his fingers. *(Pulls back Hero's fingers one by one and removes the papers from his hand.)*

MAN IN HAT: What is it?

MAN IN CAP: Some sort of papers. Memoirs . . . *(Reads aloud.)*

The Card Index

"I was born in 1920; after finishing at the village school . . . I forgot to add that I had a friend in the village school who used to give me cheese, this friend came from the village. When I finished school . . . When I received my school certificate I applied for a job with the Town Hall. In 1938 in a hotel room I polished my shoes with the bedspread. After completing my elementary schooling I went to a secondary school and after finishing at the secondary school I tried to . . ." *(Shakes his head, reads on.)* "Come to me all you people!"

MAN IN HAT: What is he doing? Is he asleep? Maybe he is pretending?

MAN IN CAP *(reads on):* "In 1938 in a hotel room I polished my shoes with the edge of a carpet and I slashed the towel when I was wiping my razor blade. Then, when I was eighteen, I faced my final exams but I had no time to sit for them because on the first of September, 1939, the World War broke out. That terrible cataclysm which swallowed . . ."

MAN IN CAP *puts the papers away in his briefcase and they both leave. A smartly dressed middle-aged man crawls into the room on all fours. He is impeccably turned out and perfectly groomed, with a knife-edge part in his hair. As if his hair has been combed from the inside. He walks around the whole room on all fours, sniffs the table legs, the chair, peers under the bed, then begins to talk, raising his muzzle toward the* HERO.

MAN WITH PART: Do you know who I am? Do you know who you are? Who he is? What he is? I have my pride. No, sir, you are too insignificant to talk to me like this. I didn't want to know, had I known I couldn't have cheated. But I am suffering. I am . . . I am . . .

HERO *shifts and sniffs.* MAN WITH PART *is quiet.*

The Card Index

HERO: I smell a stranger. I smell varnish and whitewash, farting and literature. Who's there?

MAN WITH PART *adjusts his hair and tie with his paw.*

Oh, it's you, Bobby.

FAT MAN *in glasses walks through the room. He is reading a newspaper and looks around. He is standing in the middle of the pavement. He calls* MAN WITH PART.

FAT MAN: Bobby, heel!

MAN WITH PART *rubs his muzzle against the Fat Man's trouser leg.*

Bobby, down.

MAN WITH PART *lies down.*

Dead dog.

MAN WITH PART *pretends to be dead.* FAT MAN, *smiling, takes a bone out of his pocket and throws it under the table.* MAN WITH PART *fetches the bone back.*

Bobby, beg. Good dog . . .

MAN WITH PART *begs beautifully, cocking his head to the left, then to the right, and smiles.* FAT MAN *draws out his hand.*

Paw, Bobby.

MAN WITH PART *offers his left paw and has it smacked.*

Right paw.

MAN WITH PART *corrects his mistake and offers right paw.*

(To HERO*)*: He's well trained, isn't he?
HERO *(sitting up on the bed)*: I don't know.
FAT MAN: Tell him to suffer and he suffers. Tell him jump and

he jumps. He can even read and write. Got a medal at a dog exhibition in Paris. He is intelligent and well trained . . . training isn't difficult . . . all you need is a skillful approach and a little patience . . . There are four elements which affect a dog's efficiency: his hunting instinct, the winds, his feet, and his intelligence. Bobby's got feet and he is good at sniffing the winds . . . Will you take him?

HERO: I have no money . . . doesn't he bite?

FAT MAN *(laughs):* He has no teeth, he's only got a tongue. He licks.

HERO: I'll give you a pair of socks in exchange.

FAT MAN: All right.

> HERO *takes off his socks and hands them to* FAT MAN, *who puts them in his pocket. He walks away reading a newspaper, and has quite forgotten about Bobby.* HERO *stretches out his hands and strokes Man with Part's head.*

HERO: Want a drink?

MAN WITH PART *(still on all fours):* An espresso and a brandy, please.

HERO: You drank black coffee at the previous political phase and what good did it do you? You better have some water. *(Pulls the basin full of water from under the bed.)* An honest simple man soaked his feet in this water. Drink. It's medicine for the likes of you. For the likes of me . . .

> MAN WITH PART *draws out his tongue like a dog and is about to drink the water from the basin.* HERO *laughs.*

Enough! You are civil! Stop being a fool and sit down. We'll have some coffee in a minute. Admittedly I haven't got any coffee or cups or money, but then, what are surrealism, metaphysics, and the poetry of dreams for! *(Calls.)* Two large coffees!

> WAITRESS *comes into the room. She is wearing a cap and an apron. She places a silver tray on the table.*

The Card Index

WAITRESS: Shall I undress?

HERO: That's not necessary. I hate burlesque.

WAITRESS *runs out.*

CHORUS OF ELDERS:
Tramp
trash
trainer
training
Tripolis
trollop
truism
trumpeter

HERO *and* MAN WITH PART *are absorbed in drinking their coffee. They stop drinking to examine their hands carefully, then they show their hands to each other: the right and the left. They examine them closely.*

HERO *(holding Man with Part's left hand):* Oh, there is a stain here! It's black.

MAN WITH PART: That's ink.

HERO: Ink? You could lick that off.

MAN WITH PART: Oh, you've got a stain too! Two stains! Two red stains!

HERO: That's blood.

MAN WITH PART: Real blood?

HERO: Enemy blood.

MAN WITH PART: I only know the taste of water, vodka, saliva, and ink. What does blood taste like?

HERO *(takes out a pin and pricks the finger of* MAN WITH PART, *who sucks it):* A drop of blood. How did you survive the war, the occupation? Did you ever hold a gun?

MAN WITH PART: Thanks to the wife! The wife, to the wife, in the wife, with the wife, oh the wife . . . on the wife . . . under the wife.

HERO *(shouting)*: Get lost!

> MAN WITH PART *drops on his four paws, reaches for the cup with his paw and drinks up the coffee. Enter two well-preserved middle-aged* WOMEN. *They carry on a lively conversation interspersed with bursts of laughter.*

WOMAN: I him, he me, he to you, she to him, you know what he's like, when you to him, to himmmmmmmm. *(Roars and neighs and laughs. She looks around.)* Oh, darling, there you are!

> MAN WITH PART *stands on two feet.*

My husband, my dear. This is my friend, darling.

> MAN WITH PART *kisses the other woman's hand. Smiling, full of the joy of life, he leaves with the* WOMEN. *The* WOMEN *have polish on their fingernails.*

CHORUS OF ELDERS: Corps de ballet, correspondence, cosmetics, cosmic, copulation, marmalade, marble, martyrology . . .

> HERO *is looking for something feverishly. Crawls under the bed. Opens drawers. Looks in all the corners.* CHORUS *leaves.* HERO *is alone. He is searching his pockets. At last he pulls out a length of rope and ties it around his neck. He tests the rope. Looks around the room. Searches for a nail. Goes to a hatrack. Finally he opens the wardrobe and gets inside, shutting the door behind him. The wardrobe is closed. It opens after a long pause.*

HERO: Why don't you hang yourselves? I prefer the little toe of my left foot to all of you put together. What? Go and hang yourselves! No! You love yourselves too much. That hag loves her little dog more than me, a man. Because it is her doggie. She loves her appendix more than the whole of humanity.

The Card Index

HERO *sits on the bed, pulls a bag of sandwiches out of his pocket, unwraps the paper and begins to eat.* FAT WOMAN *enters.*

FAT WOMAN: Shame! So young and already a Peeping Tom!

HERO *(stops eating)*: What are you doing here, madam? This is a private apartment. Who let you in?

FAT WOMAN: Ha ha ha ha ha ha! *(Laughs herself silly.)* Private apartment!

HERO: I don't know who you are.

FAT WOMAN: Victor, you spied on me in my bath.

HERO: A quarter of a century has passed since then! Yes, I re-member. But I see, madam, that you have now come out of the water. You can go your way now. I am busy just now, I have to read my correspondence.

FAT WOMAN: I'll wait. *(Sits down in the chair. She may start knitting a pullover.)*

HERO *(takes some envelopes from the table. Opens a pink enve-lope. Reads in a clear voice)*: "My dear Felek, I am touched by this proof that you haven't forgotten me. Do come, so that with my own little fingers I can drop in your mouth the sweetest chocolate from the box you've sent me. Yours, Bronia." *(Opens another envelope and reads.)* "Dear Henio, I hear very unwelcome news about you and about your ex-ceedingly reckless acts. Is this how you repay me for my solicitude, for my efforts and expense which I contributed to your education and upbringing? You were seen in a poolroom, a party to an incident with a bum. You don't go to lectures, you are absorbed by games, gambling, and love affairs. So this is what I have to endure in my old age. You must pull yourself together, my dear Henio, because one more bad piece of news and I will cut you off, and not only will I stop your allowance but I shall also disown you as my son. I send you my fatherly blessing, may it give you the strength to direct you in the right path. Your mother

51

is weeping. Your heartily disappointed father." *(Daunted,* HERO *crumples the envelope and puts it in his pocket. Takes out another envelope and reads.)* "Dear Cousins, the celebration on the occasion of your silver wedding anniversary causes me great joy. As a witness of your wedding twenty-five years ago, I cannot now believe that a quarter of a century has already passed since that moment when you pledged each other to push forward together the wheelbarrow of life beneath the lofty emblem of love. Twenty-five years have passed like a brief moment. May life continue for you full of roses, so that, reborn in your children, grandchildren, and great-grandchildren, you may become for them the patriarchs of those principles which you yourselves have so worthily embraced. Your old friend, N. N. Warsaw, January 24, 1902."

After reading the last letter HERO *puts on his slippers and leaves the room. He is followed a moment later by* FAT WOMAN. *Now nothing is happening on the stage. A five- to ten-minute break is suggested. The curtain may be lowered, or left hanging.*

HERO *returns after the interval. Pulls out his sandwiches from his pocket, unwraps the paper and begins to eat.* FAT WOMAN *enters a moment later. She looks around.*

FAT WOMAN: Shame on you! Such a young boy peeping at women.

HERO *(interrupting his meal):* Who let you in here? This is a private apartment.

FAT WOMAN *(laughs):* Private apartment? A private apartment!

HERO: I don't know who you are.

FAT WOMAN: Mr. Romek, you spied on me in my bath.

HERO: That was ages ago . . . Yes, I do remember. I see, madam, you have now come out of your bath.

FAT WOMAN: Mr. Bolek, I remember you as a little boy in a sailor suit with a collar.

The Card Index

HERO *lies down on the bed. His back turned to the audience, his back toward* FAT WOMAN. *She sits on the bed.*

HERO: Ages ago.

FAT WOMAN: So what? So what, my precious?

HERO *(jumps up):* You old cow, you slab of bacon, you tub of lard. I do remember. I was fifteen. It was July. The light of the setting sun in the water. A red river under the crowns of black alders. You were white and fat. You were a young bosomy wench. White as snow. Emerging slowly from the dark water. Black alders stood over the water. A red sun in their crowns. I would have given half my life, my whole life, a whole city, the whole world, to touch your breasts. If I could put my hand on your thigh, on your mons veneris.

FAT WOMAN: On what?

HERO: On your mons veneris. You idiot, you cow, you could have been my queen. You could have been music, a garden, a fruit, you could have been the Milky Way, you cow. But you kept it for some wise guy, con man, cynic, buffoon, thief. Now you're blubbering. You could have been my flame, a spring and a joy. How I suffered then. I wanted to jump out of my skin.

FAT WOMAN *is knitting a pullover!*

Because of you I nearly ended up a sodomite. Your belly was a greater revelation to me than America was for Uncle Kowalski. Your rump was a star. You idiot, you barrel of pickled meat. Run away before I crush you on the spot!

HERO *falls silent. A very lively middle-aged* WOMAN *enters the room. She runs to* FAT WOMAN, *kisses her rapturously and starts her patter.*

LIVELY WOMAN: Just imagine, my dear. Sleek-fitted watered silk, shoestring straps holding a low square bodice and a built-in bra. The back view shows a plunge line and a bow trim on

53

a horizontal strap. Black and rhinestone earrings cylindrical in shape. Gilt highlights the pastel nylon georgette and there is braiding around the low-cut bodice and the hem. Or a swoosh of silk organza over a taffeta slip. Rich gold braid around a mandarin collar, a curved bodice and sleeves. *(Jumping up from the bed and kissing* FAT WOMAN.*)* Bye-bye, you must phone, you really must . . . Bye-bye, do phone . . . remember . . . bye-bye! *(She goes out.)*

FAT WOMAN *(folding up her knitting):* So you wash your hands of me, Mr. Bolek!

HERO: I do.

FAT WOMAN: I put such great hopes in a visit to you. I thought that for the sake of an old friendship you would give a hand to a lonely woman. But you couldn't care less. What is it to you that the secretion of my gonad is increasing. Yes, Mr. Marek . . .

HERO: I told you so many times, my name is Stefan.

FAT WOMAN: Yes, Mr. Stefan. Now I often suffer from headaches, hot flushes, dizziness, and pains in the joints. I noticed that lately I have undergone slight digestive disturbances and changes in my electrocardiogram. The doctor thinks the oral use of estradiol will be sufficient, and that duoetylosty-bestrol is equally effective. But this drug gives me nausea and stomach pains, so what do you suggest in the circumstances? If it hadn't been for the fact that I have known you since you were so little *(shows how little)* I wouldn't have turned to a stranger over such an intimate matter.

HERO *(reading from the newspaper):* "The Number 5 Sugar Refinery in the Hrubieszow region was the first off the mark in this year's campaign."

FAT WOMAN: How the world has changed. People are quite indifferent to the sufferings of their fellow beings.

Children's voices are heard: "Mommy, Mommy." FAT WOMAN *leaves.* HERO, *stretched on his bed, goes on reading. Enter* CHORUS. *They sit in their places.*

The Card Index

CHORUS OF ELDERS:
> Do something, get a move on, think.
> There he lies while time flies.

HERO *covers his face with the newspaper.*

> Say something, do something,
> Push the action forward,
> At least scratch your ear!

HERO *is silent.*

> There is nothing happening.
> What is the meaning of this?

HERO: Leave me in peace.

CHORUS OF ELDERS: Thank God, he is not asleep.

HERO: Are you saying I must do something? I don't know . . .
(yawns) . . . perhaps . . .

CHORUS OF ELDERS:
> He's falling asleep, the gods will rage!
> There can be no bread without flour.
> There must be action on the stage,
> Something should be happening at this hour!

HERO: Isn't it enough when the hero scratches his head and stares
at the wall?

CHORUS OF ELDERS: That is something.

HERO: I don't feel like doing anything.

CHORUS OF ELDERS:
> But even in a Beckett play
> somebody talks, waits, suffers, dreams,
> somebody weeps, dies, falls, farts.
> If you don't move the theater is in ruins.

HERO:
> Today a flea circus is performing *Hamlet*
> leave me alone
> I am going away.

CHORUS OF ELDERS:

Stop!
HERO:

I am going away.
CHORUS OF ELDERS:

Where?
HERO:

I want to be excused.
CHORUS OF ELDERS:

He is drunk.
HERO:

Stupid bunch, let me sleep.
CHORUS OF ELDERS:

You are falling asleep again
What does it mean?
HERO:

I'll finish off all of them!

He takes a sharp kitchen knife from the table and approaches the ELDERS, who are sitting still. He pierces through two of the ELDERS and cuts off the third Elder's head. Now he lays out the CHORUS on the floor. Sits on the bed. He smiles at the audience. Washes his hands. Visibly shaken, he walks around the room. Even starts to run. Stops. Hits himself first on his right then on his left cheek. Walks up to the wall. Presses his hands against the wall.

There, you see, you fool. Go on, crack it with your head. Batter it. Where do you think you are going? Where? To that stupid woman? To the hospital, to humanity, to the refrigerator, to the salmon, to the vodka, to a pair of thighs, to a teen-age leg, to the nipple. Ah, there you are! Go on, bite your own fingers. It's good nourishment. Everything dies under your hand because you don't believe. Where do you think you are crawling, you ass? You have been crawling for the last thirty-eight years. To the sun? To truth? To the wall. I stand against the wall. My brothers, my generation, it's to you I'm talking. They can't understand us, neither the young nor the old! *(Turns to audience.)* How did it happen? I can't understand it. There were so many different things in me and I was so many different things and now there is nothing. Here. Here! There is no need! No need to cover up my eyes. *(Pause.)* I want to see right to the end.

A pretty GIRL *enters the room. Jumper. Tight-fitting trousers. Handbag, magazine, book, apple.* GIRL *walks there and back once or twice. She is what is known as "a stunner." She sits at the table. Looks at the newspaper. Combs her hair. Takes out a mirror, etc., etc. Turns to* HERO.

GIRL: I'd like a cream bun.

HERO *(as though ashamed, talking to himself)*: Well, yes, after all, why not.

GIRL: I'd like a cream bun, please.

HERO *(to the audience)*: When I was still alive . . . well, really . . . I think you will be shocked . . . you will be bored and amused by this tale.

GIRL: I'd like a cream bun and a small coffee.

HERO: Why small?

GIRL: Don't you understand my language?

HERO: Are you a foreigner?

GIRL: Meine Hobbies: Reisen, Bücher, Theater, Kunstgewerbe . . . ich suche auf diesem Wege einem frohmütigen und charakterfesten Lebensgefährten . . . ich bin vollschlank, keine Modepuppe . . .

HERO: You are German.

GIRL: Yes.

HERO: I am delighted. You see, I must explain that there has been a misunderstanding.

GIRL: Ah, so?!

HERO: You see, this is a private apartment. I live here . . . Naturally I am very pleased . . . make yourself at home. I must tell you . . . du bist wie eine Blume . . .

GIRL: So this isn't the "Crocodile"?

HERO: The young ones have no idea . . . how old are you?

GIRL: Eighteen . . . but the door was open . . . I saw various ladies and gentlemen, they chatted and drank coffee . . .

HERO *(sits at the table beside the* GIRL. *Takes her hands, stares at her face. The* GIRL *smiles):* There you are, you young ones poke fun at everything . . . Though maybe that is how moronic journalists see you . . . I have faith in you people . . . please do not laugh. I have a request to make. Allow me a few minutes. I want to tell you . . . I heard you speak German. Are you German? Yes. Actually, I have nothing interesting to tell you. Please don't think I want to seduce you, to push you into bed . . .

GIRL: Oh yes, there is a bed here. Do forgive me, I hadn't noticed.

HERO: God! If only you could understand me. It's all so simple. I will only take a few minutes and then go away, but I have a duty to tell you something and you have a duty to listen right through. I wish to say that it is good that you exist. That you are in this world of ours, just like this, that you are eighteen, that you have such eyes, lips, and hair, that you are smiling. That's how it should be. Young, with a clear bright face, with eyes that have not seen . . . have not seen. I just want to say one thing: I do not feel hatred toward you and I wish you happiness. I wish you would go on smiling like this and be happy. You see, I am covered with dirt and blood . . . your father and I hunted in the forests . . .

GIRL: Hunted? Hunted what? . . .

HERO: Each other. With rifles, with guns . . . no, no, I won't go into that . . . now the forests are quiet, aren't they? It is quiet in the forests. Please, do smile . . . In you lies all the hope and joy of the world. You must be good, pure, and gay. You must love us. We were all in a terrible darkness beneath the earth. I want to say it again: I, an old freedom fighter, wish you happiness. I wish happiness to the youth of your country as well as ours. Let's say our farewells. We shall not see each other again. I've expressed myself rather clumsily. How silly, how terribly silly. Isn't it possible to say anything, to explain to another person? It's impossible to convey what's most important . . . Oh, God!

A moment's silence. Again there is silence. An inarticulate cry emerges from the LOUDSPEAKER. *Then, more clearly, the words Aufstehen! Aufstehen!* HERO *rises. Stands to attention by his chair.* GIRL *looks at him with surprise, as if she hadn't heard the din.*

LOUDSPEAKER:
Raus! Alles raus!
Maul halten, Klappe zu, Schnabel halten!
Willst du noch quatschen? Du hast aber Mist gemacht!
Du Arschloch, Schweinehund, du Drecksack!

HERO stands against the wall. Presses his face against it. LOUDSPEAKER *grows silent.* Silence. GIRL *gets up and tiptoes out of the room. She leaves behind a red apple. A minute's silence.*

CHORUS OF ELDERS *(recites):*
Don't be afraid
this is your room
see there's the table there's the wardrobe
an apple's on the table
furniture frightens you
you silly thing
that man won't come back

You are frightened of the chair
of an old newspaper of a knock
of voices behind walls
perhaps you wish to draw attention
by your eccentric behavior

Smile
that man won't come back
look in our eyes
don't hide in corners
don't stand against the wall
no one compels you
to stand against the wall

Speak

Enter TEACHER *carrying a briefcase. He sits at the table. He takes various papers out of his briefcase. Puts on his glasses. Pays no attention to anything or anyone. He talks, he poses questions. The* TEACHER *may be played by the actor who played* UNCLE. *He has glasses instead of a mustache.*

TEACHER: Please don't be nervous. Please think.

FIRST ELDER: What are you doing here?

TEACHER: He is sitting for his final exams. His matriculation exam.

FIRST ELDER: Yes, all right, but why today?

TEACHER: He is already twenty years late. I can't wait any longer.

FIRST ELDER: What questions have you got for him?

TEACHER *(all the while keeps looking at his papers)*: Oh, various. Please sit down and get ready.

FIRST ELDER: You really have chosen the time badly.

TEACHER: What can you tell me about Poland's annexation of Ruthenia?

SECOND ELDER *hands* HERO *a cup of coffee. Leads him to his bed, helps him to lie down, and covers him with a blanket.*

FIRST ELDER: With the death of King Daniel, Ruthenia passed through a period of decline. Although one of his sons, Szwarno, being Mendog's son-in-law, did briefly occupy the Lithuanian throne, the chronicles provide an unflattering account of the other son, Lion I. His reign was followed by that of his son, Jerzy I, who united under his rule the principalities of Wlodzimierz and Halicz. His sons, Andrzej of Wlodzimierz and Lion II of Halicz, lost Podlasie and Polesie in favor of Giedymin, but subsequently entered into friendly relations with him and one of Giedymin's sons, Lubart, married Busza, the daughter of Andrzej. Boleslaw, the son of Trojden, the prince of Mazowsze, married one of Giedymin's daughters, that is the sister of Aldona, the wife of Kazimierz the Great . . .

TEACHER *(looking at his papers)*: Excellent, brilliant. Well done, young man, you are splendidly prepared for life. As a matter of fact, you've passed your exam but, to make absolutely sure, I must put a few more questions to you. You understand that this is pure formality . . . Do tell me, what have you been reading recently?

FIRST ELDER: The newspapers.

TEACHER: But what in particular?

FIRST ELDER: The personal-advice column.

TEACHER: Please describe in your own words.

FIRST ELDER: While on vacation, a certain Anka fell in love with Bolek. They used to go out together, but earlier, Bolek, who was Anka's first passionate love, used to go out with Halina, which fact he disguised from Anka, and he was taken into the army. When I sent a letter to Bolek that I was expecting a baby which was conceived earlier, Bolek did not reply but wrote to me later that he was expecting a baby from Halina, who used to go out with Tadek. My parents wouldn't allow me to go out with Marek because Bolek was fifty years younger than me. And now, dear Aunt Mary, I am sixteen and when I first knew Victor I was eight and I trusted people. Now I have lost faith in Bolek and people point at me in our little town. Please advise me, my dear Aunt Mary, what am I to do. My situation is that much worse because my mama, who for seventy years was barren, has now been cured and is also expecting a baby. What sort of life can I look forward to?

TEACHER: All the same, you young ones are all set to enjoy life. Fact, a sad fact . . . and who is to do the suffering in this world?

FIRST ELDER: That's just the problem, professor.

TEACHER: What are your plans for the future?

FIRST ELDER: I am taking up Chinese.

TEACHER: Splendid . . . and how old are you?

FIRST ELDER: Eighty . . .

TEACHER: Splendid, young man. Remember that "the child is father of the man." Thank you, I have no more questions.

FIRST ELDER *takes up his place next to his colleagues. The* CHORUS *is now sitting against the wall.*

Ah, but *(recollecting)* tell me one more thing: why do you love Chopin?

FIRST ELDER: Chopin, sir, hid guns amid flowers and has popularized Poland's name all over the world.

TEACHER: Yes, but what do you feel when you listen to his music the whole year through?

FIRST ELDER: I experience a deep gratitude to the composer.

TEACHER *(shakes his head)*: How can they say our youth is cynical and indifferent.

HERO *(sitting up and gesturing to the* TEACHER *to come over to him)*: Professor, come over here.

TEACHER *sits on the bed next to* HERO, HERO *stretching his hand, fingers apart, toward* TEACHER.

What is this, professor?

TEACHER: A hand.

HERO *(clenching his fingers)*: And this?

TEACHER: A fist.

HERO *(clenching and opening his fist)*: Hand, fist, hand, fist, hand, fist. One can use a hand to kill, strangle, write a poem or a prescription, or to fondle. *(Strokes Teacher's cheek, takes the apple in his hand.)* What is this?

The Card Index

TEACHER: An apple.

HERO *(showing him a button):* And this?

TEACHER: A button.

CHORUS OF ELDERS:

Guano	gun	glucose
Guatemala	goodies	glue
goulash	goose	glum
guzzle	gooseberry	glutton

CHORUS stops suddenly . . . is silent as though "thunder-struck." The SECRETARY enters the room. It is the same little person who earlier played FEMALE VOICE UNDER THE BED-CLOTHES. We behold rounded buttocks encased in a dress or trousers. The CHORUS gapes. SECRETARY sits on the bed and opens her documents file.

SECRETARY: These are for signature, sir.

Silently HERO signs a series of documents with his index finger.

CHORUS OF ELDERS:

Give what, tho' thou giv'st it often, is yours still,
Give what later thou wilt vainly strive to fill
When wrinkles plow this face, and at last
The glass show thy gaze that youth is past . . .

SECRETARY *(laughing):* I adore Kochanowski.

CHORUS OF ELDERS:

Be not shy, dear, thou knowest well the tale:
When the cat grows older, the stiffer is his tail;
An oak, too, when withered, parched and dry—
If its root hath life—will stand up high.*

SECRETARY: There is a journalist outside under the window, he would like an interview.

HERO: Tomorrow.

---

* Two fragments from Jan Kochanowski (1530–1584) —*Tr.*

SECRETARY: He's been waiting a whole year; you see, sir, in our time speed of information takes precedence, agencies await the latest news, developments and gossip . . .

HERO *(to* TEACHER*):* You will excuse me, I am very busy.

TEACHER *gets up but turns back in the doorway.*

TEACHER: One last small question. Could you lend me a hundred zlotys? No . . . ? Ciao, bambina! *(Goes out with his brief-case.)*

SECRETARY *(yawning and stretching):* I am so tired and sleepy. I'll get into bed. *(Gets into bed and settles down to sleep.)*

The room becomes a pavement and there are people walking along the pavement. A gentleman with a briefcase, then a young couple who stop, look around, and kiss long and passionately. Two middle-aged women speak quickly while walking: "Meat, of meat, to meat, from meat, oh meat, with meat, meatless." They pass. Enter Hero's parents. MOTHER *puts her finger to her lips. They stop over the bed.* FATHER *glances at his watch.*

FATHER: Yes, it certainly is time!

MOTHER *looks knowingly at* FATHER.

You see, Franek . . . we must have a chat about certain . . .

MOTHER: Tadek . . .

FATHER: You see, Tadek, today I want to have a man-to-man talk with you. As you know, time passes . . . I'm sure you've noted certain disturbing changes in your organism. Your beard is getting coarser and thicker, hair is falling out of your head, your voice is growing deeper . . . I am sure you sometimes have dreams, then you wake up and think about various things . . .

MOTHER *(with feeling):* Do you remember, Kornel, not so long ago you were showing him the little window through which

64

the stork had dropped him into our flat . . . we mothers are a wretched lot . . .

FATHER: You see, my child, the purpose of life is to maintain life. The most primitive type of life is sexless reproduction. Reproduction comes about through division or blossoming. An individual normally splits into two parts or he develops a kind of blossom which after a while drops off to form a new individual.

MOTHER: You never told me about this.

FATHER: The virgin conception among plant lice is notorious. No less interesting is the parthenogenesis of vorticels.

CHORUS OF ELDERS:

King
kink
kiosk
kipper
kiss
kirk
kitchen

FATHER *(looking at his watch)*: Well, you can't expect me here and now to produce a detailed description of the external mechanism of love in all the species of animals. It would take too long and in any event would be tiresome and uninteresting. Among crickets the male possesses a musical apparatus, while the female is endowed with an auditory organ which is located on her bare feet. Similarly in the case of grasshoppers, except that only the male can emit sounds. Are these sounds love calls?

MOTHER: I have no idea.

FATHER *(looking at his watch)*: "Don't put off till tomorrow what you can do today . . ." The best you can do is not to think about silly things.

FATHER *bends over the sleeping* HERO, *kisses him on the forehead. Parents leave.*

HERO: Pity you were asleep. Father was saying interesting things.

SECRETARY: So you've got a father? How strange.

HERO: And a mother.

SECRETARY *(laughs)*: Ha ha ha ha ha ha ha.

HERO: What are you laughing at?

SECRETARY: I can't imagine you as an embryo. So you were as small as my little finger?!

HERO: Yes, just as small . . .

SECRETARY: And then you were breast-fed?

HERO: I was bottle-fed.

SECRETARY: And you dropped little golden lumps into the pottie?
. . . And what about your mustache? When did you start growing a mustache and a beard?

HERO: On Monday.

SECRETARY: What a deep voice my little cockerel has . . .

HERO: Poor Father . . .

SECRETARY: Poor? Tell me about your old man.

HERO:

Had my father
been a captain of a ship
a bishop
if he had a saber a star a ribbon a stool a crown
had he discovered America
conquered a peak
in a word
had he differed at least a little
from ordinary average people

SECRETARY: My dearest, people are not average!

HERO:

. . . had he been different
from these ordinary average people
had he been a cannibal
a Lollobrigida
an astronaut

But he was an insignificant clerk
in a small provincial town
he was like me
like you
like all of us

Such people depart quickly. One forgets them. You will leave here and you will forget me. Isn't that so? You are already forgetting.

SECRETARY *takes the apple in her hand.*

When I was a little boy I dreamed of being a fireman. I wanted to have a shining helmet, a belt, and a hatchet. I imagined carrying a little girl I knew out of a burning house with everybody admiring me, thanking me, and pinning a medal on me. I ran around the courtyard with my arms outstretched *(opens out his arms and imitates engine noises)* and then it seemed to me that I was an airplane and a pilot. I was also a tiny foal . . . When I started school my dreams changed, I wanted to be a traveler, a millionaire, a poet, or a saint.

SECRETARY: And now?

HERO: Now I am always myself. I traveled a long way before I reached myself.

SECRETARY: Yourself? And how are things over there? What is there?

HERO: Nothing. Everything is on the outside. And there are faces, trees, clouds, the dead . . . but all this merely flows through me. The horizon narrows down constantly. I see best when I close my eyes. With eyes closed I can see love, faith, truth . . .

SECRETARY: I know nothing about that.

HERO: Yes, that is how it is . . .

SECRETARY *(giving him the apple):* Eat it . . . tempt yourself . . . He is asleep . . . Men are terribly childish. They are always pursuing something, and when they at last arrive at their

67

goal, they despair. They are in a hurry, they murder. A seed would never have grown inside them. They are careless. None of them is capable of protecting a fruit for nine months. It's lucky it's we who carry and give birth to life . . . They are born abstractionists. There is death in that. *(Sits on the bed and, smiling, begins to eat the apple.)*

CHORUS OF ELDERS *(loudly)*:

He who in childhood cut off Hydra's head . . .

SECRETARY: Shhhhhhh . . . quieter . . .

CHORUS OF ELDERS *(declaiming in a whisper)*:

Will in his youth the blood of Centaurs shed,

Will rescue victims of the Demon,

Will gather laurels up in Heaven.

SECRETARY: Leave him!

CHORUS *fold up their chairs and leave the room on tiptoe.* SECRETARY *looks at herself in a mirror. Various people pass through the room. Some are in a hurry, some walk slowly. They talk excitedly, they read newspapers, call their children, exchange greetings. A young couple kiss and walk on. A* JOURNALIST *enters. He walks through the room, returns, looks around as though he were looking for an apartment number or an unfamiliar house. He moves upstage to the center of the room and stops by the bed in which* HERO *is sleeping.* SECRETARY *pays no attention to* JOURNALIST. *She takes the arm of the first available passer-by and leaves the room.*

JOURNALIST *(lights a cigarette. Walks about the room. Stubs out the cigarette. Grips the* HERO *by the arm)*: I say! I say, sir!

HERO *utters inarticulate sounds.*

Please wake up, it's me.

HERO *(sits up in bed)*: What? Who?

JOURNALIST: It's me. I must put a few questions to you.

HERO: You? To me?

The Card Index

JOURNALIST *(takes a notebook out of his pocket)*: Your secretary
    has doubtless mentioned . . .

HERO: You from the press? Haven't you seen an apple here?

JOURNALIST: No.

HERO: Perhaps you've eaten this apple . . . from the tree of knowl-
    edge of good and evil?

JOURNALIST *(laughing)*: No, I haven't eaten it.

HERO *(thinks)*: These aren't the only tricks you people are cap-
    able of . . .

JOURNALIST: I want to talk seriously. With the approach of the
    New Year, our Agency wishes to conduct interviews with
    various celebrities and with ordinary . . .

HERO: Simple . . .

JOURNALIST: . . . exactly, with simple citizens.

HERO: Well?

JOURNALIST: Could you tell me your aim in life?

HERO: I have already achieved it and now it's rather difficult to
    say . . .

JOURNALIST: And are you glad to be alive?

HERO: Yes . . . no . . . yes . . . in fact, yes.

JOURNALIST: And why?

HERO: How should I know . . .

JOURNALIST: Then who should know?

HERO: I have no idea.

JOURNALIST: And is there anything you still wish to achieve?

HERO: Well . . . I have various plans, I would naturally wish . . .
    although . . .

JOURNALIST *(writes it down—thinks—suddenly asks)*: What are
    your political views?

HERO: Who's got political views at five in the morning? The
    guy's mad. He wants me to have views at dawn! One has to
    wash, dress, relieve oneself, brush teeth, change a shirt, put
    on a tie, and pull up one's trousers, and only then is it time
    to have opinions . . .

JOURNALIST: I see . . . Do you believe in salvation?

HERO: Yes . . . no . . . that is . . . up to a certain point . . . funny question.

JOURNALIST: If I'm not mistaken, you are an ordinary person?

HERO: Yes.

JOURNALIST: Do you know that you hold the fate of the world in your hands?

HERO: Up to a point.

JOURNALIST: What do you intend to do to maintain peace in the world?

HERO: I don't know.

JOURNALIST: Do you realize that in the event of nuclear warfare humanity will perish?

HERO *(almost gaily)*: Naturally, naturally.

JOURNALIST: And what are you doing to prevent the explosion?

HERO *(laughs)*: Nothing.

JOURNALIST: But surely, you love humanity?

HERO: Naturally.

JOURNALIST: But why?

HERO: I don't know yet. It's difficult to say, it's only five in the morning. Perhaps if you drop in around midday I might know.

JOURNALIST *(puts his notebook away)*: I haven't learned much here.

HERO: You've come too late.

JOURNALIST: Goodbye.

HERO *is silent.*

GONE OUT

••

CHARACTERS

HENRY

EVE

GIZELA

BENJAMIN

OLD MAN

YOUNG MAN

STRANGER

MALE AND FEMALE VOICES

DANCERS

FIRST LADY

SECOND LADY

SERGEANT

TWO AMBULANCE MEN

FAT MAN

ACT ONE
TABLEAU ONE

A large room with a variety of clocks, all of which have stopped. Each one shows a different time. In the corner there is a green palm and a comfortable armchair. A newspaper is lying on the floor and next to it a pair of well-worn slippers. A table and chairs. A Woman, her face buried in her hands, kneels in front of the armchair. We can see the nape of her neck. Light lies still on the taut white skin. On one of the shelves there is a figurine or perhaps just a wooden block painted black. One of the clocks starts and then stops again. The Woman talks indistinctly, then sounds turn into words, but we hear only some of the words and sentences.

EVE:

lord I am not worthy
I am not
no

A pause.

I will not touch thy robe
why do you hide
you are afraid lord
you run away
lord only say the word
and my soul shall be healed

Pause.

what "lord" what "soul"?

Gone Out

lord? I don't know your lordship
what is your lordship doing here?
lord you see into my heart

Pause.

I am yours my lord
an idiot
an old woman, my lord

*The Woman's back begins to shake with sobs, then she gets
up, we see her face; she is laughing, but we also notice signs
of tears.*

what am I saying
she wants the lord does she?
I am talking to the lord
to the wall
oh lord lord lord
but you are not there!
pity

Now the Woman is speaking clearly.

I have made a vow that if he comes back
to me I shall never to the end of my life
I shall never to the end of my life -
to the end of my life I shall fast
I shall
each Saturday I shall
maintain silence

if he returns
and if he does not return what shall
I eat—sweets?
I my lord, thy vessel
thine
why was Jairus' daughter worthy?

Reflecting.

Jairus? What Jairus?

A clear VOICE *is heard on the radio.*

VOICE: Attention please, there is a special announcement. In the early hours of this morning . . . he left home . . . and did not return . . . here is a description . . . height, face, eyes, nose . . . he was dressed . . . anyone who can give any information about the missing person is requested . . .

The announcement is followed by dance music, then silence. The Woman gets up and walks about the room.

EVE: "Eat something" . . . they say to me . . .
MALE AND FEMALE VOICES *(heard from various sides):* Eat something, eat something, eat something, eat.
EVE:

    I can't eat
    I can't swallow anything
FEMALE VOICE:

    She really can't swallow
    anything
EVE:

    this house this furniture
    these odds and ends
    made sense
    only in connection with him
    it was he who
    filled this armchair
    these slippers
    me
    with himself
FEMALE VOICE:

    it was he who filled her with himself
EVE:

Gone Out

it's not only I who wait for him
my body does too
I mean
not only my soul
but also these hands
lips

Pause.

what use is this hand if he is not touching it
it is only a limb
it is a tool for gripping carrying washing up
what use is my face
what use is it to you

*Turns to the audience and in the course of her monologue
gradually comes forward.*

she is an old crumpled shell
in the eyes
of this or that student this or that
booking clerk passer-by rent collector
only for him
has my face an inner side
is young
to you my face means nothing
it is one of the million faces
in this city

MALE VOICE:
this old face means nothing to us
it is one of a million faces in this city
one of a hundred million
an average face
of an average woman
meaning nothing
or meaning little

EVE:

only he can take my face
see it once again
in a bus in a crowded train
with a drop of light on its cheek
That was in a cellar
during an air raid
that was in the field beneath the clouds
in the forest
I was twenty
I was sixteen
I was thirty

Shuts her eyes, listens . . .

MALE VOICE:

your face beneath the sky
with eyes shut
rain fell on it
and she lay smiling
asleep
a bird sang around her eyes and lips
it nested in the corner of her eye
leaves fell
about the rosy shell of her ear
the sea roared on the sands
and then your face
began to close
then turned away it fell
into the sand
then your head revealed
the other side
covered in hair without a mouth blind
I felt it under my palm
it grew
full of weeds pine scent dampness

77

in the cellar
buried under white lime-dust
pressed and torn apart
with holes for eyes
with a rat's face
giving birth to man
giving birth to humanity
a huge face
with huge tiny
lips
your evil face
giving birth
and then through all the lines
furrows
light began to flow toward me

VOICE *fades. The Woman stares at the white blind clock faces.
Talks to herself as though she were remembering something
with difficulty.*

EVE:

today I swallowed time
these clocks tick in me
in my
in my throat
belly
in my underbelly
in my heart
in my stomach
they tick in me harder
louder
heavier
the clock hands enter
into me
pierce me

now these clocks tick
in the joints of my hands
they tremble in my knees
they tick in my thighs
they tick in my hair
they tick in me
in mine
they go deeper
it's not true I am talking about the weather
I am talking about him
it's not true I am talking about dresses
I am talking about him
it's not true I am talking about the weather
I am talking about his lips

FEMALE VOICES *(variously pitched, repeat)*:

it's not true she is talking about dinner
she is talking about him
it's not true she is talking about the weather
she is talking about him
talking about herself she talks about him

Pause.

EVE:

I have nothing to talk about
when I do not talk about him

She walks over to the table, touches its surface with her fingers and examines them.

how dusty it is
how much dust is gathered here
I must kill this time
I must somehow kill this time

FEMALE VOICE:

she must somehow kill this time

EVE:

I will read

FEMALE VOICE:

she will read

EVE:

I will answer letters

FEMALE VOICE:

she will answers letters

EVE:

I will phone

FEMALE VOICE:

she will phone

EVE:

I will fill this time with something
I will find a way of filling this time

FEMALE VOICE:

she will fill this time with something

EVE:

I will be busy from morning till night
I will be a father to the children
I will sew on a button
I will dust
I will have a manicure

*She turns to the armchair. She sits "enthroned" in it, quite
still, her arms stretched along her body.*

I feel sand
running through my windpipe
the sand grates against my teeth
time seeps from
the upper half
of my body
through some vessel
into the lower half
and lower
still

She speaks in a tired, sleepy voice.

now I feel like a queen
the queen of hearts
who has two heads four breasts
two upper halves
touching each other
but lacking that other half
the lower half
the part essential for
a mother the world the male
for the hive
I am a paper queen
I have a head here and there
alas
this is fatal for a simple
woman

*Lights slowly fade. They come on and fade again. In the
darkness there is only one source of red bloodlike light whose
intensity fluctuates.*

TABLEAU TWO

*A herd of "suitors" bursts upon the stage. They dance a courting
dance. Something like a ballet in which amateurs and understudies
jostle alongside excellent dancers. They are both young and old.
The young ones are in tights. They represent distinguished-looking
civil servants, soldiers, athletes, and clerks, as well as petty provincial officials carrying briefcases and wearing light overcoats.
The lights come on and off, on and off. The suitors carry flowers,
ostrich feathers, strings of pearls, and colorfully woven cloths.*

Sometimes they laugh, squeak, bellow, neigh like stallions, and grunt.

Two men in dinner jackets stand in the corner of the room. They offer cigarettes to each other and whisper in each other's ear. In the silence the light grows in intensity. The suitors are now gathered around something and are examining it, bending over it, sniffing. They are very quiet now, as though we were seeing them in a dream. Some of the dancers are dressed in skins of dogs and baboons. They wear dog and monkey masks, others wear glasses. The baboons have pink and violet bottoms. One of the suitors is picking at lice in his fur. Two others bite each other in silence. One of them is licking another on the face. The light dims. In the darkness the eyes, teeth, and the pink, moist, protruding tongues and the baboons' bottoms shine with greater intensity. We hear quickened, guttural breathing. The light continues to dim. The suitors run off the stage in silence. The lights come on again. The last one to leave is a drooping figure in a light coat and carrying a large yellow leather briefcase. He blinks as though surprised, looks back, lifts his hat and leaves. EVE *lies with arms outstretched in the middle of the room. She rises slowly. Sitting on the floor, she stretches herself, yawns, and stretches her whole body once more.*

TABLEAU THREE

Full daylight. Scene as in Tableau One. EVE *is lying on the floor, her hair disheveled. She wakes up, stretches herself, yawns, sits up, and looks around.*

EVE: It's very stuffy in here. What's that pungent smell? Stinks like a stable, sperm and phosphorus. Hair everywhere, cigarette butts, socks, matches. I have such a heavy head. Such a weight of dreams. Never before have I carried such a burden. *(She gets up, looks at the white clock faces and goes over to the mirror, in which her whole body is reflected.)* Oh God, I am bruised all over. *(Examines her reflection.)*

my body
he shouldn't go out
he shouldn't leave me like that
he shouldn't leave my body alone
my corpse
these shackles
dig into my flesh
it struggles
I begged him don't go
he left me
he left my body
I shall wait for him
eternally young
but my body will grow old

Two elegantly dressed LADIES *enter the room. They sit at the table as though it were a table in a café. They look at* EVE. EVE *hasn't noticed them. They don't exist for her. One of them touches the table with her white-gloved hand and examines her dust-covered palm.*

I shall wait for him
LADIES *(together):*
she will wait for him

Amused.

she will wait for him

Seriously.

will she wait for him?

83

Gone Out

EVE:

>But my body
>doesn't want to wait for him
>it changes hour by hour
>it moves away
>
>it doesn't know the past
>it doesn't remember itself young
>this body stretched over me
>worshiped derided
>this body doesn't remember
>it's only I who am remembering
>what am I to do now
>what am I to do with myself

FIRST LADY:

>what is she to do now?

SECOND LADY:

>what is she to do with herself?

She lights a cigarette.

EVE:

>he would have found a way out
>something to do
>he would have filled my day
>put the books in order write that card
>sew on a button
>stuff a teddy bear
>water the flowers
>polish the silver
>bathe the dog wash your hair
>have a look at Sartre
>sew on a button? what is a button
>if there is no eternal life
>what do I care about a button
>if there is no salvation

what good are buttons to me
does the other world exist?

FIRST LADY:

she wants to know whether the other world exists

SECOND LADY:

the other world does not exist

EVE *goes to the palm and carefully wipes its leaves with a
cloth.*

EVE:

no one will believe me
that I am a mature woman
that I sometimes think about immortality
and in the most unexpected places too
in the shop for instance
sitting at the table after lunch
or in the kitchen
can one think about the soul
while one is seasoning the soup

LADIES:

yes one can

EVE *(touching the palm leaves)*:

don't laugh at me
here I am a forty-year-old woman

FIRST LADY *(to* SECOND LADY*)*:

she is forty-five

EVE:

here I am a forty-year-old woman
I wish to be saved after death
perhaps I will be an angel
lord! will I rise from the dead?

FIRST LADY:

naturally, like all of us

EVE:

oh, lord, my lord, when the trumpet sounds

Gone Out

    will the gravestone lift
    and my young body
    emerge from the earth
    pure
    like a mountain crystal
    will my thighs rise from the dead
    will my breasts
    rise from the dead
    my lips the skin of my neck
    funny questions
    will my hair rise from the dead
    lord I ask you
    funny questions funny and stupid questions

FIRST LADY:

    My lord, she is asking you
    funny and stupid questions

SECOND LADY:

    will her dyed hair
    rise from the dead

The LADIES *get up and leave the room.*

EVE (*covering up the mirror*):
    if he doesn't come back in an hour
    if he doesn't come back at once
    I will tell the police
    perhaps he

Clutching her throat.

    he had no cause
    surely he has not done himself
    any harm

A slim seventeen-year-old Girl enters the room with a light dancelike step.

. . . he drank his coffee changed his pants

changed his pants drank his coffee
said nothing
behaved normally
surely a man who changes his socks and shaves
has no intention of . . . leaving this world . . .
unless he is English or a Lutheran
. . . how silly I am

The Girl kisses EVE *on the cheek.*

GIZELA: Isn't Daddy back yet?
EVE: No.
GIZELA: Maybe something unexpected turned up.
EVE: I don't know. Quite frankly, I'm terrified . . .
GIZELA: That something might have happened?
EVE: Father went out and disappeared.
GIZELA: What do you mean, disappeared?
EVE: I don't know . . . he's simply not here.
GIZELA *(embracing her mother)*: Daddy always comes back.
EVE: You were the last one to speak to him.
GIZELA: In the morning . . . I noticed nothing special. He kissed
　　me and asked what time I would be back . . . I saw he took
　　a clean handkerchief . . . Mother, surely a man would not
　　think about a clean handkerchief who . . . really, you have
　　no reason to worry . . .
EVE: I don't know. I phoned the ambulance, the radio, the tele-
　　vision, the office . . .
GIZELA: We just have to wait . . .
EVE: We can't wait . . . This time I'll phone the police.

*She phones and says something. Puts the receiver down. At
that moment a police* SERGEANT *arrives and salutes.*

SERGEANT: Is this the address where a citizen has been reported
　　missing?
EVE: Yes, my husband . . . Do sit down.
SERGEANT: Please describe the incident.

Gone Out

EVE: My husband . . .

SERGEANT: Please relax.

EVE: He has disappeared without a trace.

SERGEANT: Please give a description of the missing person.

EVE: I'm so sorry . . . I've simply lost my head . . . everything's gone out of my head . . . I can't remember . . . perhaps my daughter . . .

SERGEANT: That's unfortunate. *(Salutes and turns to* GIZELA.*)* Well, then, maybe you . . . ?

GIZELA: Well, really, Daddy was quite nondescript, that is . . . similar to . . . what I wanted to say . . . he wasn't like anything . . . he was like everybody . . .

SERGEANT: Yes.

GIZELA: I don't know. I never looked at Father carefully. Daddy is fair-haired. Wears glasses.

EVE: What on earth are you saying? Father has blue eyes . . . You know, Inspector, when people are together all the time they don't notice niceties of features so much.

SERGEANT: And what about special marks.

EVE: I haven't noticed anything special. It all rubs off after so many years.

GIZELA: It all rubs off, Mommy . . .

EVE: It's the second time in my life that I've had to describe him, you understand, Inspector . . . *(Aside.)* What is he like? The first time I described him in detail was twenty years ago. To my best friend . . . now I have to describe him to you . . .

SERGEANT *(sitting down):* We'll do all we possibly can.

EVE: Perhaps you'd like a cup of tea. I'll collect my thoughts.

SERGEANT: Sorry, I'm on duty.

GIZELA: Don't go yet. With you being here everything is less terrible.

SERGEANT *(taking off his cap):* I'm sorry I keep coming back to the same thing, but I forgot to ask about a certain important detail concerning the missing person.

Act One Tableau Three

EVE: I won't hide anything from you . . .

SERGEANT: Something's just come into my head.

EVE: Doubtless you want to know what the relations between us were like lately . . . Gizela, leave us alone . . .

GIZELA: Mommy, you're forgetting that I'm grown up.

SERGEANT: What I want to know is what type of frame did your husband's glasses have?

EVE: Gizela, please leave us.

GIZELA leaves, frowning.

SERGEANT: You will forgive me, madam, for asking about such a trifle.

EVE: I won't hide from you even the most intimate aspect of a mature woman's experience . . .

SERGEANT: God forbid.

EVE: I will not hide from you that our relationship . . . *(Telephone rings.* EVE *picks up the receiver.)* Yes. No. Yes . . . he hasn't turned up . . . *(Covers receiver with her hand.)* That's his mother . . . *(Talking into the receiver again.)* No, I don't know what to do next . . . Yes, I know you are his mother . . . No, you have no right to speak like that . . . I'm sorry . . . I wanted to ask about a trifling detail. Do you remember what kind of frame Henry had? Of what? Of his glasses . . . yes . . . he didn't wear glasses? I'll phone you . . . we're waiting . . . *(Replaces receiver.)*

SERGEANT *gets up.*

What was it I wanted to . . .

SERGEANT: Please relax.

EVE: You've put a very important question to me.

SERGEANT: Oh, that's nothing, it's merely a formality.

EVE: I know, but I will do everything I can.

There is a knock.

GIZELA: May I come in?

SERGEANT *(finding it difficult to make himself heard)*: Because what we are concerned with is when did the missing person leave the house?

EVE: He shaved and drank his coffee, changed his socks . . . *(Grabs* SERGEANT *by the hand.)* Surely a man who shaves in the morning with such care can't go out and do himself any harm? You're experienced in these matters. Please tell me.

SERGEANT: I assure you, madam.

EVE: Well?

SERGEANT: We are concerned to know how many days the missing person has been away from home.

EVE: What did you say?

SERGEANT: How many days is it since your husband left home?

EVE: Today.

SERGEANT: Please relax. We want to know when he left the house for the last time.

EVE: Today at 7:30. He changed his socks, drank his coffee.

SERGEANT *(wiping forehead with handkerchief)*: At what hour and on which day did your husband leave the house?

GIZELA: He took a clean handkerchief . . .

EVE: Today in the morning.

SERGEANT: What do you mean "today"?

EVE: Just like any day, except holidays and weekends.

SERGEANT: At what time does he normally come home from work?

EVE: At five.

SERGEANT: Never later?

EVE: On one or two occasions he got back at seven.

SERGEANT *(looking at his watch)*: It's now eight.

EVE: Eight?

SERGEANT: In other words, your husband is an hour late.

EVE: An hour?

SERGEANT: One hour.

EVE: I don't know; I've stopped counting the hours.

SERGEANT *puts on his cap, salutes, stands at attention, shrugs his shoulders, and leaves.*

One hour.

GIZELA: There, you see, Mommy. *(Kisses her.)* I'll take Cleopatra out for a walk. She must want to go.

The bitch Cleopatra is heard squealing. GIZELA *takes the leash and leaves. After she is gone all the clocks begin to go; then, one by one, they stop.*

AN INTERLUDE

An open space on the outskirts of the town. Perhaps a cemetery, perhaps a refuse dump. Grave diggers or maybe municipal garbage collectors. One old, one young. One fair, one dark. They are eating pineapples and bananas and drinking water from a bottle. Spades, pickaxes, boards, ropes, bones, tin cans, and stuffed rats are lying around on the frozen earth.

OLD MAN: The earth is frozen two feet down.

YOUNG MAN: Maybe even three.

OLD MAN: You won't bite it without a wedge.

YOUNG MAN: If you can't bite it, you'll have to lick it. *(Laughs.)*

A middle-class Man approaches along a little avenue, rubs his spectacles with a velvet cloth and looks at the little heap of earth and at the tiny burrow which the grave diggers have dug up.

STRANGER: What are you doing here, good people?

OLD MAN: Blowing into our hands.

STRANGER: This isn't much of a hole.

OLD MAN: Oh, if you push it in well . . .

YOUNG MAN *(with a broad laugh):* Then you can push in even the biggest one . . .

STRANGER: It's no larger than a mouse hole.

OLD MAN: That's only a beginning . . . This tiny hole will change into a big hole, into a pit . . .

STRANGER: Has someone important died in your town?

OLD MAN: No, he hasn't died, only . . .

YOUNG MAN *(with a broad laugh):* . . . only he's been born again.

OLD MAN: He's had a resurrection. Almost come back from the dead . . .

STRANGER: If he's just been born again, why are you digging him a grave?

OLD MAN: To keep warm, sir.

STRANGER: I know something about this business. You go on. *(Turning to* YOUNG MAN.*)* You look the more stupid, there's honesty shining in your eyes.

YOUNG MAN: Chaff.

STRANGER: What's that about chaff? The old man's hiding something in the chaff?

YOUNG MAN: Gaff.

STRANGER: Eating bananas, eh? You are doing quite well.

OLD MAN: Here in the south, sir, bananas are as common as beans and cabbage.

STRANGER: Who is departing from this world? Is it a secret?

YOUNG MAN: And what's that to do with you?

OLD MAN: Where have you come from? Who are you?

STRANGER: From far away, from Paris. Have you heard of the place?

YOUNG MAN: Paris, kiss my ass. *(Silly laugh.)*

STRANGER:
Who am I?
I who am
the something which I am not
and I am not that which I am

OLD MAN: See here, brother, nobody's departing, only arriving.

STRANGER: Arriving?

OLD MAN: Like the rosy-fingered dawn.

YOUNG MAN: You wouldn't like a bun, madam? *(With a silly laugh, he peels a banana.)*

OLD MAN: We're making trial drills . . . looking for oil, sir.

STRANGER: Are you hoping to get oil out of this man's remains?

YOUNG MAN *(sharply)*: A toady lies here.

OLD MAN *(nudging YOUNG MAN in the ribs and speaking quickly)*: Yes, a daddy lies here. Shut up, you bastard. Did you speak, sir? Are you a daddy too, perhaps?

STRANGER: Did you say a toady lies here?

OLD MAN: A daddy.

STRANGER: A toady who was a daddy?

OLD MAN: You are wrong there, sir.

STRANGER: So here lies Daddy who was a toady . . . hell! If he is lying there, what are you looking for in that frozen earth? Let him rest in the Lord.

YOUNG MAN: . . . and light eternal. But what lord? He was an atheist.

OLD MAN: An order's come from Caesar; we've got to dig, sir. We've got to help him. Otherwise he won't rise from the dead.

YOUNG MAN: We've got to search.

OLD MAN: There'll be a ceremony in memory of the deceased. There'll be an artistic performance, then a funeral. There's been a provocation in this ancient town. But this is an old tale . . . grass grows on it now.

YOUNG MAN: Gaff.

STRANGER: What did you say, young man?

YOUNG MAN: Chaff.

OLD MAN: He was a noble gentleman, loved people, flowers, even loved human beings.

STRANGER: So you have an order to dig out Daddy who was a toady.

Gone Out

OLD MAN:
> What's in a name? That which we call a rose
> By any other name would smell as sweet.

YOUNG MAN: He was a good man, but bad men invented a false
> tale, forged the dot over the "i," rubbed out a comma,
> and went on quoting
> it in this form
> they dug a statement out of him
> from his chest
> breaking standing orders and bones
> he sang like a canary
> hanged himself with his own rope

STRANGER: So it was he who sang?

OLD MAN: When they played a tune on his teeth he not only
> sang, he danced as well.

YOUNG MAN: Now truth will out.

OLD MAN: And he, the poor stump of truth, will out of the earth.

YOUNG MAN: Truth will shine in the world.

STRANGER: Go on digging and look sharp. You must get him out
> of this hole quickly. Let the rays of the sun light up the
> error.

OLD MAN *(indulgently)*: My dear friend . . .

YOUNG MAN: You've got fiery blood, sir. Every inch a Frenchman.
> A real dandy.

OLD MAN *(to* YOUNG MAN*)*: Light a fire, the earth will warm up.
> My tongue will loosen up in the warm. The world will melt
> like frozen shit. The gentleman here doesn't know our cus-
> toms.

STRANGER: The dark one is telling tall stories.

OLD MAN: Sit down and listen. Listen and sit down. *(He lights a
> pipe.)* We're digging slowly because experience tells us not
> to hurry. Since morning we've had the messenger here
> twice running and giving us contradictory orders. We started
> work on this bed at midnight . . . The hole was very tiny,
> a finger's depth, and then the messenger rushes up . . . Go
> on, Antek, you tell him the rest, I'll take a nap.

YOUNG MAN: The envoy, sir, had steam billowing out of his mouth. "Bury it, bury it quickly," he says, "so that the eyes won't see any trace." But why? I ask. He gave me a terrible look. He whispered. He spit in my ear: "Let this degenerate specimen get lost and rot. That dog, that crook, murderer, swine, and provocateur. The prosecutor has presented fresh evidence. They found forged documents today and a new truth flows out of them for us . . . Bury it and stomp it down: there is nothing lying here." So right away Bamba and I, we covered up the hole. That old dark one, his name is Bamba, even though he's been washed in baptismal waters. So we covered up the hole and stomped it down well. Uncle stuffed his pipe . . . he's no uncle of mine, but I call him Uncle because I'm an orphan, sir, and an orphan without an uncle in the world is like a tiny finger. So I call Bamba Uncle. "Let's go," says Uncle, but again there's someone rushing toward us from over the gate, his tongue hanging out. "Brothers," he says, "listen, brothers, everything's changed, there's a mistake which we'll put right. We have to dig up the martyr's body, we have to commemorate this murderer." And so he babbles, sometimes he says "martyr" and sometimes he says "murderer." You could see he was so frightened his tongue got twisted, poor thing.

OLD MAN: He who dies of fright gets a farting funeral.

STRANGER: The only fear I know is the existential fear, when the essence is too weak and existence has no taste.

YOUNG MAN: "There's been a mistake," he says to me. "We'll put up a statue. He was no nigger. Never touched a woman. Someone else raped Grandma. He was a white man and so were his ancestors. But they talked him into it, so he turned dark all over. And black he lies in the earth, although he was wholly white. Now we'll give justice to the ashes and tomorrow a funeral for the bones. The family which had cut him off from its trunk like a rotten member is now adopting him as husband, son, brother, and daddy." But that's an old tale. He is rising from the dead.

Gone Out

OLD MAN:

> I stood over the grave, my mouth open wide,
> there was something and there was nothing inside;
> but I see, sir, this wearies you and you balk
> at the truth of ordinary, dim, simple folk.

> I say to the messenger: "Orders is orders, sir." He went
> away, quickening his pace, while we got back to work dig-
> ging up the bed. And you, where are you from?

YOUNG MAN: That's enough from you, old man. The gentleman
from Paris has told you already that in his shadowy existence he's lost the taste of the essence. Now he walks about
the world begging for bread and, like every French atheist,
he's winking at God.

OLD MAN: Godspeed, good sir! I'm going to dig other pits; the
little angels are waiting their turn. You've got to shove the
white little angels into the ground before they begin to stink.
Such is the fate of flesh . . . *(Walks away.)*

YOUNG MAN: Uncle has hidden . . .

STRANGER: Yes, tell me . . . Here, here you are . . . *(Takes some
beads out of his pocket.)* Go on . . .

YOUNG MAN: Uncle hasn't told you there is nothing in this grave.

STRANGER: What?

YOUNG MAN: We've dug right through the night and no go.

STRANGER: Nothing?

YOUNG MAN: Nothing. Seems nothing was buried here.

STRANGER: But they want to dig something out.

YOUNG MAN: That's the orders. When in Rome, do as the Romans
do.

STRANGER: I don't understand what's going on here. It's like some
cadaverous pantomime.

YOUNG MAN: You travel a lot but you don't see nothing. Yes,
when it comes to it, sir, you are very stupid.

He spits into his hands and takes hold of a spade.

ACT TWO
TABLEAU FOUR

A ten-year-old boy with a satchel on his back enters the room.
He is pale and disheveled but good-looking. Takes off his satchel
like a sack and throws it on the floor.

BENJAMIN *(walking about the room and talking to himself):*
   . . . childhood
   the childhood years! he! he! he!
   they talk so much about this happy childhood
   about children, the only heavenly inhabitants of earth
   who after death swell the host of little angels
   well I am a child
   and so what

   adults waste my time
   first they played with me as if I were a little monkey
   threw me up in the air
   till once I fell and got bruised

   Father used to tell me fairy tales
   about dwarfs they kept beating me
   on the paws
   well take Mom as an instance: what was talking to her like?

   year in year out
   from morning till night:
      wash your hands
      have you washed your hands
      your hands are grubby
      don't eat with your hands

97

Gone Out

don't wave your hands like that
take your hands out
sometimes I say to myself
well cut those hands off and that will be that
they never talk seriously to one
when I was little
they treated me like a little dog
they invented strange words and lisped
even now one has to wait months and months
for a sensible answer

all of them are always dissatisfied with one
one would like to know something
about politics metaphysics astronomy
all one hears is "stop picking your nose"
you ask them about demographic policies
about population explosion
and instead of an answer they give you
chitchat about spinach
but these are things that concern me to the quick
go—they say—go and play
don't sit around with adults

there is no peace even in the toilet
the moment I get in there
right away somebody is calling what are you doing in there
    so long
what were you doing in there
get out at once
wash your hands
remember you mustn't play with your ding dong
that's what the penis
is called in our family—
don't play with it you will become an imbecile
sometimes whole days pass

and you won't hear anything sensible
from the adults

Enter EVE.

EVE: Ben, what are you doing under the table?
BENJAMIN: I'm not doing anything.
EVE: Don't be rude.

BENJAMIN *comes out and stands politely by the table.*

Look at your hands.
BENJAMIN: It's ink. I've been working.
EVE: Go and wash your hands.
BENJAMIN: Yes, Mommy. *(He goes out with a grim expression.)*
EVE: Poor children. Deprived of a father . . .

A knock on the door. Louder. The door opens. Two AMBU-
LANCE MEN *lead in a man with a bandaged head. The
bandage covers the whole face, giving the head the appearance of an egg.* EVE *stretches out her hands as if she were
at the same time pushing the patient away and pulling him
toward her. The* AMBULANCE MEN *place him gently in the
armchair. One of them hands* EVE *a wire spectacle frame.*

This . . .
FIRST AMBULANCE MAN: It's the spectacle frame. Found where the
    accident occurred.
EVE: This . . .
SECOND AMBULANCE MAN: The husband. The documents all tally.
    Please check.
EVE: Him?
FIRST AMBULANCE MAN: Please relax, the danger is over. During
    his walk your husband stumbled or rather slipped on a ba-
    nana skin and fell. As he fell he hit the base of his skull
    against the head of a statue. He has also suffered scratches
    on the face. Apart from the injuries, the fall has resulted in
    a shock . . . The doctor . . .

SECOND AMBULANCE MAN: The speech cells in the brain have not been destroyed, merely blocked. The doctor on duty has diagnosed that the shock will pass and that the patient will recover his speech within forty-eight hours.

FIRST AMBULANCE MAN: The patient's memory is at the moment functioning in response to stimuli. On his own he can't recollect anything. Please leave the patient in peace. Don't tire him and don't ask him any questions.

EVE: What I don't understand is where the bananas come from.

SECOND AMBULANCE MAN: Please relax.

EVE: I've never seen a banana skin lying about anywhere in the streets.

SECOND AMBULANCE MAN: Well, madam, you get some fool who eats a banana and throws the skin on the pavement.

EVE: Thank you, gentlemen, thank you from the bottom of my heart.

FIRST AMBULANCE MAN: Oh, it's nothing, madam. Will you please be kind enough to certify the delivery . . . Yes, please sign just here.

EVE: Does he take any food?

SECOND AMBULANCE MAN: Only liquid. The patient will not be able to eat any meat, bread, or fruit for the next two or three days. At the moment he is not able to think logically.

FIRST AMBULANCE MAN: It will all pass after a good sleep.

> EVE *kneels in front of the armchair and touches the sleeper's hand with the tips of her fingers. The* AMBULANCE MEN *look at each other, smile with understanding and sympathy. They leave.*

TABLEAU FIVE

The patient is sitting in the armchair which has been placed next to the palm. He has his slippers on his feet. The bandage has been partly removed so that one can see his eyes and lips. EVE *comes into the room with a small red watering can and waters the palm. She turns to her husband. A serious tone is maintained throughout the scene.*

EVE: Are you going to the meeting tomorrow? *(She is watering the palm. She takes no notice of the patient's silence and continues to question him in a lively tone.)* The doctor said you could go back to work tomorrow. Why don't you say something? *(She comes close to the patient and looks into his face.)* Do you hear me, Henry?

HENRY: I do.

EVE: So why don't you answer my questions?

HENRY *(as though he were trying to recollect something and this is causing him difficulty. At last he says with relief):* Why are you calling me Henry?

EVE: What should I call you?

HENRY: I beg your pardon?

EVE *puts away the watering can, sits opposite* HENRY *and takes him by the hand.*

EVE: Henry, tell me what's your name.

HENRY *does not reply.*

How old are you?

HENRY *does not reply.*

101

What's your profession?

HENRY *does not reply*.

What's your religion?

HENRY *does not reply*.

How much do you weigh?

HENRY *does not reply*.

Are you married?

HENRY: What does "married" mean?

EVE: Oh God!

HENRY: I beg your pardon?

EVE *(terrified)*: God . . . "I beg your pardon?" I didn't really
mean . . .

HENRY: What does "God, God" mean?

EVE: I'll explain that later, Henry. But now try to remember
what country you are living in, and what town.

HENRY *moves his head in a negating gesture*.

Do you know what you're doing here under this palm?

HENRY: I'm conversing with you.

EVE: Have you got any children?

HENRY: Children?

EVE: Yes, children. Have you got a son, a daughter?

HENRY *does not reply*.

Gizela!

GIZELA *runs into the room. She jumps onto her father's knee
and embraces him*.

GIZELA: Daddy, Daddy!

HENRY *(embarrassed)*: What does "Daddy" mean?

GIZELA: Mommy, what is he saying?

HENRY: What does "Mommy" mean?

EVE *(controlling herself, speaks in a matter-of-fact voice)*: I am Mommy, you are Daddy, and this is our child, our daughter.

HENRY: I am delighted to meet you.

GIZELA: How funny you two talk. *(She gets off her father's knee.)*

EVE: Daddy has forgotten that we all form a family.

HENRY *gets up and moves to the door.*

And where are you going?

HENRY: I? I'm leaving.

EVE: You can't go now, you have to sit and listen to what your wife tells you.

HENRY *(politely)*: Yes, madam. *(He sits in the armchair.)*

EVE: So you don't remember my name?

HENRY: No.

EVE: Why then, simply call me "darling."

HENRY: Darling.

EVE: So there you are, darling!

HENRY: So there you are, darling!

GIZELA *(almost in tears)*: What does it mean? Why are you tormenting me in this way?

HENRY: I'm hungry.

EVE: Hungry? What would you like?

HENRY: A carrot . . . no, wait a minute . . . ham, I think . . .

EVE: Gizela, go to the garden and bring father a carrot or two.

GIZELA *leaves.*

And what do you intend to do now?

HENRY *(looks at her, smiling)*: What am I to do? I don't know.

EVE: Have a little sleep, that will do you good.

HENRY *looks at her with a smile.*

You poor thing! *(She pats him on the head.)* You miserable little thing. *(She goes out.)*

HENRY *(writes something on the floor with his finger and talks to himself)*:

103

happy
unhappy
happy unhappy

He thinks for a moment.

I am happy
happy *(crying out)* happy!
EVE *(rushing into the room):* Did you call me?
HENRY: I am *(in a singing tone)* happy, happy, happy!
EVE *(with determination):*

You're wrong!
you must have forgotten
what I told you last night
surely I have explained
why you are so very unhappy
HENRY *(stubbornly):* I am happy.
EVE: Have you forgotten who you are?
HENRY: No.
EVE: Then listen, my poor wretch.

HENRY *regards his wife with a smile;* EVE *takes him by the hand.*

You were an unwanted child. Your father already had six sons and pined for a daughter. Long before you were born he chose Elizabeth as your name. When your mother found out in her seventh month that it was going to be another son, she was so frightened that she lost her speech. You were born prematurely. It was only thanks to the doctors that your life was saved. During the first few years your mother dressed you like a girl and called you Lizzie. Your father worked so hard he didn't even notice. Anyway, your father's case wasn't very clear either. As a matter of fact, he was found during stock taking in a supermarket. Someone left him behind in a shopping basket. Unfortunately, his origins were never settled. Blood tests revealed gypsy blood mixed with pure alcohol of unknown provenance. At that time they started building hotels and restaurants designed solely for Mohammedans and vegetarians. Your father lived happily with that psychological hump on his back. One day, however, he entered a bar where he was attacked by a certain white man with a bottle of dark ale. Struck on the head, he ran out of the bar and never regained his senses.

HENRY *smiles and nods.*

I won't describe to you how unhappy you were at school. You will hear all that from your school friend whom I have just cabled to come. I wish to tell you about some very intimate things . . .

Enter GIZELA, *who places a basket with carrots next to the armchair and gazes affectionately at her father.*

You were a very timid, shy, and clean boy. You passed your childhood amid old calendars and newspapers. One day, when you were a five-year-old little monkey, you were playing with matches. You knew that children who play with matches wet their beds at night—you lived under a constant threat of that catastrophe—but you played on until one night it happened. You woke up and you felt cold and damp below. Then quite independently of Kierkegaard whom you did not then know, you became acquainted with fear and trembling. You stood naked in the face of IT and several years before the contemporary French philosopher you distinguished essence from existence. That was a moment of illumination which recurred in your life only once . . .

HENRY *reaches into the basket for a carrot and begins to nibble it, not like a human being, but like a rabbit, a hare, or a mouse.*

That moment of the deepest experience recurred fifty years later in Debrecen, where you found yourself on an Orbis vacation tour. Again you felt clearly and terrifyingly, as you had when you were a little boy, the separation of essence from existence. Years later you had the opportunity to talk about this privately with the French philosopher, whose wife was so impressed . . . Do you remember?

HENRY *(nibbling the carrot, mumbles)*: I don't remember.

EVE: All right, then. Let's reach deeper.

GIZELA: Mommy, stop. Look, he really is happy.

EVE: You are too young to understand.

GIZELA: But he is . . .

EVE: He is not happy. And if he is, we must immediately make him aware of the tragic situation in which he finds himself. Don't you see that he can't be happy? He is an adult, not an oaf or a poet. After all, he has to prepare a lecture for tomorrow, and his career depends on it. Everything depends on that lecture, our whole future . . . Don't you understand that? We must make him arrive at a point where he's capable of knowing the correct chain of events . . .

HENRY *has stopped nibbling the carrot and listens, his head tilted slightly. There is a mischievous flicker in his eyes, and something like understanding.*

. . . and to achieve this he must move from sensible to abstract general knowledge. What's the use if he acknowledges me as his wife, if he doesn't appreciate what the consequences are? We must clarify for him the laws and obligations which arise out of the relationship of husband toward wife. The obligations of a father . . . *(She takes away Henry's carrot and throws it into the basket.)* So you see, my poor wretch . . .

GIZELA: He isn't a poor wretch at all. It's a long time since he's had such a happy expression . . . At last he is free, really smiling. He's no wretch, Mommy.

EVE: But he will be. Can't you see that he must become what he was in order to be what he is? Don't you understand that if

106

he won't be what he was then he will be what he was not?
He will simply be nothing. And this I will not allow!
can't you see Gizela
that he wants to leave home before lunch
he comes and goes
but he doesn't know why
I will bring him down to earth
I will take him by the hand like a child
like a little puppy
I shall bring him to the place where he used to be where
      he raised his family
where he lived where he's done his dirty work
where he did beautiful and ugly things
—in the last resort it's all the same—
I will bring him to this little nook
and he will have to sniff it
and when he sniffs it he will remember
and understand . . .

      But all of you must help him. We have only forty-eight
hours, Gizela. Where personal, intimate matters are concerned—the whole work of the body, love, and the kitchen—
I will reconstruct him from his foundations. But I have no
head for politics. You are younger, Gizela, you do politics
at school; you must take care of that side. I must go and
prepare lunch. Yes, child, everything must be as usual. No
changes. At home nothing has changed . . . do you understand? Now go and remind him about all those sociologico-
political problems. About political systems, about the road
to socialism, to capitalism, to feudalism. In other words,
make him conscious of the world he lives in. Remember that
for the time being Father's memory functions in response
to stimuli. And don't forget either that you are his daughter.
You may of course now and again throw in a few words on
the relationship between daughter and father, what a father
means to his daughter, what a daughter means to her mother.

(Intends to leave the room, but stops in the door, thinking, then returns.) Gizela . . .

GIZELA: Yes, Mommy?

EVE: I'll strike the iron while it's hot. Lunch can wait.

HENRY *(nibbling his carrot)*: I am very, very content.

EVE: Gizela, leave us now.

GIZELA *(looking beseechingly at her mother)*: Please don't do him any harm! *(She strokes her father on the head and leaves.)*

EVE *(walking slowly about the room.* HENRY *has now finished his carrot and follows her with his eyes)*: Well, whatever you may say, you've no right to forget that you suffered, that you were very unhappy at school, in the army, during your holidays. Even your name was awful. Hoopoe, or something like that. Stinks like a hoopoe. Those birds apparently smell pretty bad. You've changed your name. You call yourself Lavender. But people always smell out everything. Let's stop all this nonsense, Mr. Hoopoe. *(She stops in front of her husband.)* Look at me carefully. Does anything strike you?

HENRY: No.

EVE *leans over him and whispers in his ear. She breaks off, examines his face, and again leans over to whisper something.*

EVE: And now?

HENRY *shrugs his shoulders.*

I was young, gay . . . When you met me in the dentist's waiting room I was a vain happy young thing in love with life, and now I am almost old and almost an unhappy woman. That's what's left of me after twenty years. No, this is madness! *(Aside.)* No, I can't tell him what my body was like twenty years ago. *(She goes over to a built-in closet and*

108

*opens it. Old and new suits hang on hangers. She pulls out
a black worn-out dress suit.)* Do you remember this?

HENRY *examines the old suit.* EVE *takes the trousers in her
hands.*

Look at these pants. They are like a topographical map. How
many years have you spent in them with me by your side?
How many good and bad moments, how many disappoint-
ments and exultations? How many government crises in
France! Don't you remember a terrible scene of jealousy in
these trousers on Lake Balaton? Take them in your hand.
Sometimes an inanimate object says more than a host of
choirs. There are tears in the heart of things . . .

HENRY *takes the trousers in his hands.*

You gaze at these pants as if they were an exotic plant or
the flag of a toy kingdom. And yet you've passed your man-
hood in them. You've left a particle of your soul in them.
They were with you step by step at receptions, weddings,
funerals. One mustn't despise one's clothes . . . They are a
part of our organism and our personality. We are born
naked. They are our wrappings and we are the stuffings.
Birds, cats, and rabbits don't wear clothes. They grow out
of their organisms, out of their chemical substances. We too
grow hair, but how many hairs do we have? One can't call
them a covering.

*During this passionate speech the husband carefully exam-
ines the old trousers. He looks at them against the light
which shines through the worn-out seat.*

Remember those concerts, conferences, banquets, break-
downs, crises, jubilees, anniversaries, blunders, excesses of
power, fiascos, inflations, dinners . . . Give me those pants.
(She takes the trousers from him.) I remember when you
came from a funeral reception . . . What am I saying, you

came from a party at the embassy. It was just before midnight. "What a pity about that sauce!" you said to me in bed after midnight. I got up. Your trousers were stained at the knee with something greasy and you were quite drunk . . .

HENRY *takes the trousers from her and holds them like a seer who has been given an object belonging to a missing person. He remembers something with effort. The broken sentences and words which he utters seem to flow from a very far distance, from a deep well of memory.*

HENRY:

Colbert sauce
Genoese fish sauce
Calves' brain sauce . . .

EVE *is watching his face intently and prompts him.*

EVE: "Soubise" sauce, very thick, goes with lamb cutlets or artichokes . . . Bechamel sauce? This sauce must be quite thick so that it doesn't pour but has to be laid on with a spoon. Goes with fish or cauliflower during Lent. You dilute it not with chicken broth but with milk or fresh cream . . .

HENRY *makes a despairing gesture.*

Sauce Madeira? Sauce hollandaise? Say it, say it . . . A sauce to go with tongue?

HENRY: A gray sauce?

EVE: Yes, of course, gray . . . You do remember?

HENRY *(repeats):* A sauce to go with tongue . . . gray . . . no.

EVE: White truffle sauce . . .

HENRY: To go with boiled beef?

EVE: Oh God!

HENRY: What did you say?

EVE: Later, later I will explain everything. Also this bit about the Creator. For the moment let's stick to the sauce. We mustn't

110

let go of this sauce . . . We'll use the sauce as a stimulus . . .
You were at the embassy then.

HENRY: Knockwurst in mustard sauce à la Sierzputowski?

EVE: White caper sauce.

HENRY: Caper sauce?

EVE: But of course!

HENRY: What?

EVE: Melt butter and stir in flour, taking care not to burn. Blend
well with stock. Chop and add capers, lemon juice, and rind,
and season to taste. Let simmer for ten minutes . . . make
sure the sauce is thick enough . . .

HENRY *presses the trousers against his chest. A* VOICE *comes
over from the loudspeaker.*

VOICES:

Der Ausserordentliche und Bevollmächtigte
Botschafter . . . A l'occasion de l'Anniversaire
de Sa Majesté le Roi . . . de . . . de . . . de . . .
Le Ministre de la République Bim Bom et
Madame . . . Zefirina prient Monsieur
Henry
Henry!
Henry!! Hoopoe . . .
de leur faire l'honneur de venir à la réception . . .

BALLET SCENE

*Lights fade, come on, and fade again. In the half-light, as in
a waking dream, the stage begins to fill with guests in formal
dress. Dinner jackets, uniforms, ribbons, stars, gowns, tiaras,
smiles, and bows . . . Light grows and with it the clamor of
voices. There are both white and colored guests. Diplomatic*

111

moves, cutting ripostes, puns, succinct analyses of the international situation, aphorisms, earrings, busts, backs, bald heads . . . We hear snatches of sentences.

. . . pas semblable . . . votre métier est infernal . . . poetry is the feast of the intellect, man is a thinking reed, Fourierism, she sells sea shells, will you have a banana, madam, e sempre bene, e pur si muove, entre nous soit dit . . . eat thou honey, because it is good . . . I went by the fields of the slothful and by the vineyard of the man void of understanding . . . use your life while you can, my pussy cat, are you keeping it for the children . . . ?

The stream of words flows and glistens amid the lights, the bodies of men and women move with unusual grace, their movements are light and well timed.

These insubstantial, exquisite conversations are accompanied by music on the harp and English horn with its soft melancholy sound (being a fifth lower than that of an ordinary oboe) . . . words, lights, and music fade . . .

When the lights come on again, there are now sumptuously decked tables set against the walls; the buffet shines and glitters with silver, it is opalescent with wines, vodkas, and liqueurs . . . snow-white tablecloths . . . in a word, the author's (limited) language is not only incapable of describing, but doesn't even dare to sample, this culinary orgy . . . Let the producer unleash his imagination.

The great door is closed. Sound of horns in the silence. ("Horn" comes from "Waldhorn," i.e., a forest horn. A brass instrument developed out of a bison's horn, first employed as a sacred instrument—cf. the "shofar" used in synagogues—and to play the

112

hallali *closing a successful hunt. Brass horns were also used by stage coachmen.)*

A force like an unseen battering ram strikes the closed doors: once, twice, three times. The doors creak and eventually burst open under the pressure of this elemental power and the stage fills with guests in formal dress. This scene takes place in glaring light. Not a word is spoken. The same people who a moment ago moved with exquisite grace, who respected the autonomy of their own and others' bodies, who weighed every gesture and every word, now mob the buffet. The horns sound. The first line of guests falls and is followed by succeeding waves treading over the sprawling bodies. The scene is like a whirlwind—or panic in a burning theater. If I were to say that this scene is reminiscent of Michelangelo's Last Judgment *in the Sistine Chapel, that would be a gross exaggeration. In the first place, Michelangelo did not include a buffet and did not dress his people in official uniforms (even the most perceptive spectator will not spot there a sauce dish or crystal champagne glasses among the twisted bodies). But, above all, in such a crowd one cannot distinguish the sinners from the saints, the damned from the saved. Such folk beliefs are here almost completely obliterated. As not everyone has had the chance to see Michelangelo's work, I will compare the storming of the buffet to Matejko's painting of* The Battle of Grunwald. *In the general melee there is an occasional flash of a knife, a hand, or a fork . . . And yet the participants aren't starving. The psychology of crowds. (My picture is not a condemnation either of the capitalist system or of petit bourgeois morality!) But let's return to the stage and to factual details. What role (in all this) is played by the sauces? In what sauce is everything happening? The stage reveals the imagination of the author, who comes from an (exceptionally insignificant) white-collar family! Caviar, salmon, tongue in Malaga . . . "peacocks and bananas upon the king's table . . . !"*

113

Meanwhile, they are swarming over the buffet like ants. In the silence one hears lips smacking, hissing, scraping and the crunching of bones. They are fighting—an eye for an eye and a tooth for a tooth ... A distinguished-looking elderly gentleman loses his false teeth in a sauce boat (this isn't funny). The scene changes into a ballet. The huddled crowd covering the buffet now moves like the rump of a piebald butterfly larva. Synchronized movements of rump and feet. And the ladies' gowns, their hairdos, breasts ... in what sauces and caviars are they dipped? From this crowd, this jumbled pulsating pile, our "hero" HENRY (née Hoopoe) crawls away to the side in a crumpled dinner jacket. He stands against the wall and wipes the sweat off his brow with his hand and clears his ear of (red) caviar. His trousers are stained with a thick white sauce. It is white caper sauce.

Lights fade and the gentle, melancholy, soft music of English horn and harp is heard again. From the infernal swarm (amid complete silence) comes a thunderous voice. "Man is a thinking reed" (etc., etc.). The producer may throw in a handful of aphorisms, witticisms and diplomatic (?) expressions—the author doesn't have anything at hand at the moment.

TABLEAU SIX

EVE *is walking about the room. It is midday.*

EVE:
>stimuli
>our only hope is stimuli
>we have to stimulate him
>with these stimuli
>unceasingly

114

like a bull with its horn
stimulate Henry
until struck
he will come to his senses
to me
to the family
which despite the crisis
is the basic cell in society
I will not allow the disintegration of this cell
is the family today exposed to greater dangers
    than in the days of our parents and grandparents
yes there are more pussies gnawing at the roots of
    this cell
now it is pussies in the past it used to be grisettes
    cocottes trash
no my kitten
this isn't wedding time
your wedding's behind you
now you have responsibilities
in this cell
which you have yourself called to life
so far they haven't invented a better form
Henry! Henry!

Echo repeats "Henry! Henry!" . . . HENRY *comes in and
stares at his wife with surprise.*

My dear! A certain fund of general information will allow
you to return to active life. Just as a few days ago, you are
again a full member of society. These momentary and re-
grettable disturbances are passing, and in accordance with
the diagnosis you will be able to return tomorrow to your
lecture and go on that business trip with your delegation. I
am sure no one will notice any changes or relapses. But man
is not only homo sapiens . . . homo faber, homo eruditus,
homo politicus, estheticus, or ludens . . . My dear Henry, stop

115

picking your nose, the nose is not meant to be played with. Adults should pick with the corner of a handkerchief or a piece of absorbent cotton. Man is a being of spirit and body. He is, one might say, homo sexualis . . . no, that sounds clumsy, let's say homo . . . homo . . . well, you see, Henry, the human body is something like a temple of divinity and is not indifferent to what is done with it or in it. Hymen places certain mutual responsibilities on the husband and the wife . . . Do please stop playing with your ear. However, let's move on to generalizations, to knowledge derived from the senses. Let's begin with parts of the body. If you will not recollect what you are made of, you will not know what use to make of these parts. We must learn, my dearest, to find our way through the formation of the human body and its specific parts using observation and touch, remembering at the same time that these are, apart from measuring it, the two chief methods of examining the anatomy of a live human being.

HENRY *(suddenly in revolt)*: I do object to this! Please don't remind me of anything. I want to have a free flight! Why do you torture me with what Mrs. X said about me in 1938? Or that stupid story about razor blades. I have shed the old skin, I am white and pure. I want to fly high and far . . .

EVE: Relax, darling.

HENRY: But, darling, here is an opportunity for me to forget and start again from the beginning.

EVE: The beginning is an illusion—there is only an end.

HENRY: What I have heard from all of you about myself is neither interesting nor attractive. This isn't even a biography. This is some hoary old joke brought to life again. When I talk about the beginning I mean that I can now relive my life once more from the beginning.

EVE: You can, but with us. With me, with the children, with Mommy . . .

HENRY *(roused)*: Me!?

116

EVE: You won't be able to go to the office if you're in such a state.

HENRY: All superstitions come from the bowels. The thing is to be sedentary for as little time as possible and not to believe in any thought which wasn't born in the fresh air or during spontaneous movement . . .

EVE: And what are these theories, may I ask?

HENRY: The patience of the hams—I have already said it once— is the true sin against the Holy Ghost.

EVE: Sitzfleisch was always your Achilles' heel, but that is no reason to despair. Please sit down. All these theories may be all right for geniuses but we must look after our petty affairs. So let's start with parts of the body. Please stand facing me and repeat every word after me.

HENRY *obediently stands facing his wife.* GIZELA *enters smiling.*

GIZELA: May I come in?

HENRY: Good morning, pretty miss.

GIZELA *(laughs):* Have you made any progress, Daddy?

EVE: He has realized that his place is in the cell, that is, in the family which is the cell; that he can fly high but must take his whole family with him.

GIZELA: You are overtired.

EVE *(claps her hands):* Henry! Let's begin.

HENRY *claps his hands.*

I will mention the names of the various parts of the body and you will repeat. Each time I mention a part, I will touch with my hand the appropriate part of my body or your body and you will do the same. Of course, we can do it the other way round. That makes no difference. The head—caput.

HENRY: The head—caput.

EVE *takes Henry's head in her hands.*

117

EVE: This is a head. *(She rubs her forehead as if she were re-membering something, then recites a fragment of the poem "Glimpses" from Rozewicz's* Forms.)

This is the head of the family the head of the world
so long has this head been the right hand the left leg
this poor head was
this head was a stool a shell a seat
a box a pulpit an amoeba a tribune a catalogue
a wardrobe a waiting room a magazine
this head has been filled stuffed loaded choked
with the categorical imperative imitation imperialism
import rapport
impotence inscription insurrection intention
idiom . . .

GIZELA *(shaken):* Mommy! You are delirious.

EVE:

my head my husband's head
seen for the first time
in a dentist's waiting room
or maybe it stood in a line
for whipped cream in the ice-cream shop
let's return to the stimuli!

She touches in turn the various parts of her body.

Neck—collum

HENRY:

Neck—collum

EVE:

Trunk

HENRY:

Trunk

EVE:

Limbs—membra

HENRY:

118

Limbs—membra

EVE: Gizela, please leave us alone for a moment.

GIZELA *goes out.*

Belly

HENRY:

Belly

EVE:

Navel

HENRY:

Navel

EVE:

Loins

HENRY:

Loins

GIZELA'S VOICE: May I come back now?

EVE: Not yet.

Pelvis

HENRY:

Pelvis

EVE:

Mons veneris

HENRY:

Mons veneris

EVE:

Flanks

HENRY:

Flanks

GIZELA'S VOICE: May I come in now?

EVE: Yes, but don't interrupt us . . .

The upper extremities

HENRY:

Upper extremities

EVE:

Arm elbow forearm thumb digitus minimus

HENRY:

Arm flanks mons veneris hand thumb digitus maximus

EVE: Once again.

Arm elbow forearm hand thumb digitus minimus

HENRY:

Arm elbow forearm hand thumb digitus minimus

EVE: Gizela, leave us for a minute.

GIZELA *goes out.*

Chest. Bosom pectus

HENRY:

Chest. Bosom pectus

He touches his wife's breasts.

EVE *(her voice changed):*

Breast—mamma

HENRY:

Breast—mamma

EVE:

Nipple—papilla mammae

HENRY:

Nipple—papilla mammae

GIZELA'S VOICE: May I come in?

EVE: Come in. *(Her voice is now under control.)*

The lower extremities

HENRY:

The lower extremities

EVE:

Thigh—femur

HENRY:

Thigh—femur

EVE:

Knee

HENRY:

Knee

GIZELA: Will I have to go out now?

EVE *(thinking it over)*: No, stay.

The back of the knee

HENRY:

The back of the knee

EVE:

Shin calf ankle

HENRY *(quickly)*:

Shin calf ankle

EVE *(quicker)*:

Face eye nose tip of the nose

HENRY *(quickly)*:

Face eye nose tip of the nose

EVE *(quickly)*:

Mouth upper lip corner of the mouth tongue

She sticks her tongue out.

HENRY:

Mouth upper lip corner of the mouth tongue

He sticks his tongue out.

EVE:

Teeth—dentes

HENRY:

You have forgotten the lower lip.

EVE: So, after all . . . ! Henry . . . ! Gizela, we've won! Unaided, Daddy has remembered his own lower lip! In time he will remember everything. The lot! Gizela, leave us for a minute.

GIZELA *kisses her mother and father and goes out.*

And now, darling, let's pass on to the parts of speech . . .

HENRY: Is that strictly necessary for an adult?

EVE: Most certainly, darling. He who lives must talk, he who talks must know what use he is to make of the various parts

121

of speech. First, we shall talk about the grammatical peculiarities of the feminine gender.

TABLEAU SEVEN

HENRY *is walking about the room. He is wearing a black jacket, pajama pants, and a pair of shabby old slippers. He is holding some notes in his hand. He stops in front of the mirror, adjusts his tie, smooths his hair, and begins to talk to the mirror . . . He is talking fluently, quickly and clearly, now and again consulting his notes. Here and there his face is covered with plasters.*

HENRY: Our Single-Family Homes Building Society is planning next year to build houses out of straw bricks and coffee dregs with a living area of three square feet. Experience of past years has shown that the development from monogamous families to polygamy is not only a general occurrence, but also that it is socially harmful. And in this connection our technicians and moralists have reached the conclusion that smaller dwellings will serve better the cause of tightening the bonds between the several members of the family. Under such conditions there will also be no place for jealousy which arose in feudal times. The shape of the cross-section of the joint will prevent the hardened mortar from falling outside. Our Society has called upon experts to examine the durability of the straw bricks which might be employed to construct the cell called "family" . . . the hand press of engineer Boboli has fairly wide application in the molding of family bricks . . . in order that the family should preserve the shape it takes while being pressed, the members of the family should be tied together with paper string or wire. We shall also find instructions in the Book of Genesis. The well-known idealist philosopher Bertrand Russell has declared that the nuclear arms stored throughout the world *(laughs)* have already achieved an explosive power equal to hundreds of millions of tons of TNT. In order to use up this arsenal, it would be necessary during the next 146 years to cause daily explosions of nuclear power equal in explosive power to all the bombs and missiles used during the Second World War . . .

Due to this potential danger, although I can assure you that there will never again be war, nevertheless, in connection with this possibility of explosion of stored-up material, our Society is employing straw bricks in the construction of ceilings. Such a new ceiling used by us, that is, a "naked" ceiling, will successfully withstand tremendous atmospheric pressures. A specialist abroad has said that the source of jealousy lies in the urge to monopolize feelings, in the desire to have exclusive possession of the beloved person. This feeling originated during the formation of classsociety and the transitions from polygamy to monogamy which is seen as an archetypal cell of private property . . . but as soon as this feeling arose it became subordinated to that logic of the evolution of the feelings which was born under the system of private property. In other words, man treated woman as if she were his chattel, not allowing anyone other than himself to possess her . . .

The abolition of private ownership of the means of production has lifted marriage out of its sordid condition. Practice proves that families with many children are—in the majority of cases—happy families cementing the love of husband and wife, a love which grows from year to year . . .

He stops and tears a plaster off his face. GIZELA *and* BENJAMIN *enter on tiptoe and sit quietly near the armchair.* GIZELA *is holding a book and* BENJAMIN *a cage with white mice.*

Cement is bluish-green in color or dark gray with a

bluish tint or white with a greenish tint. In principle the color of the cement has no influence on quality, only the binding power of the cement influences the durability of the concrete. In its dry condition cement behaves neutrally. However, after a time cement loses some of its binding force although, as I have already remarked, it is the basic material in the production of roof slates and ridge tiles with which we cover the individual family nests in the single-family homes. It will not be out of place here to point out the theologians' views on matters of the cell, that is, the family. The fundamental instructions for the family and the frames within which it realizes the aims of humankind we shall find in the Book of Genesis. They are:

One, "It is not good that the man should be alone."

Two, "Therefore shall a man leave his father and his mother, and shall cleave unto his wife: and they shall be one flesh," and

Three, "Be fruitful and multiply."

Naturally one should not use stale cement in binding. That is why, on receiving a consignment of cement, one ought to note the date when it was poured into the sacks. Stale cement is no longer a material of full value because it loses about twenty per cent of its binding power.

It is against these conditions that we must on each occasion measure the family structure. The social significance of marriage and of the family nest is the subject of our inquiry which has shown that we may use straw bricks to insulate the walls of family nests. If, however, we wish to insulate a building affected by damp, then naturally we must remove the damp. It follows, therefore, that marriage may be a successful struggle against loneliness. A man and a woman may operate a hand press for the production of straw bricks but they achieve mutual knowledge only through love . . . For it is only in the flesh that people arrive at the full realization of their personalities.

HENRY *sticks a plaster on his forehead and continues.*

The press employed in the manufacture of straw bricks consists in principle of a base, a fixed frame, a movable frame, two pulleys, chains, and other elements, including a wooden hammer, a sieve for the cement, a box for the cement mixture, a molding press, a frame, and a measuring cone for checking the thickness of the clay suspension.

During the production of flat tiles normal apparel—that is, a white linen coat buttoned up the back—is obligatory. The sleeves of the shirt and the coat ought to be rolled up above the elbows. White caps. Women should wear head scarves. Rubber gloves are not generally used.

When laying ordinary roof slates we fill in the ridge grooves with mortar and animal hair. When laying tiles on the roof, start at the bottom and work your way up. Slop basins make for cleanliness both on the table and on the floor. As far as laying out a body is concerned, it should in principle be laid out on a special table or tray with a protruding edge all around . . . the body laid out flat is supported on two wooden blocks, one underneath the shoulder blades and one underneath the pelvis. Flat tiles are laid out in the same way but without mortar. In order to insure the insulation of the covering, we tuck in flax fiber dipped in tar. The skin, fat, etc., which have been extracted in the process are at once placed in dishes. The flax fiber . . . flax dipped in the slop basin . . . (HENRY *is rubbing his forehead. He has forgotten . . . tears a plaster off his forehead and speaks slowly.)* The flax . . . flax . . . *(trying to collect his thoughts).* Toadflax—linaria vulgaris, round-leaved toadflax—linaria spuria . . . sharp-pointed toadflax—linaria elatine . . . pale-blue toadflax—linaria repens . . . perennial, smooth . . . corolla violet with dark lines and yellow palate . . . flowers July to September . . . ivy-leaved toadflax—linaria cymbalaria . . . with egg-shaped leaves . . . hairy . . .

sandy cornfields . . . July . . . *(He stops, sits down in the armchair and repeats, mumbling.)* . . . bastard toadflax . . . thesium humifusum . . . bastard toadflax—humifusum . . . toadflax . . . bastard . . . bastard . . .

HENRY *covers his face with his hands and sits in silence for a while. He puts his hand on Benjamin's head and talks quietly but clearly.*

I feel I am departing
I don't want to leave you without a blessing
but I don't know how it's done

BENJAMIN: You've still got a temperature . . . Mommy was saying that you are coming to your senses.

GIZELA: Slowly coming to your senses.

HENRY:

I would have wished to bless you
but I honestly don't know how our father did it
it's disgraceful that there is no manual of some sort . . .

BENJAMIN *shifts about because he is uncomfortable under his father's heavy palm which rests on his head.*

I wish . . .

BENJAMIN: Don't force yourself, Daddy, we know you have nothing to say. That's only natural.

HENRY *(stubbornly)*: I wish to leave you with certain directives . . . True enough, no one has sufficient experience in these matters . . . Your grandpa fell into a well when he was drunk and had no time to compose his last will and testament. He had no time to transmit to me anything of his great experience. I find myself in a more fortunate situation and I wish to transmit to you that which your grandpa had no time to transmit to me.

GIZELA: Then transmit it to us, Daddy . . . *(She shifts about on her chair and looks intently at her father.)*

HENRY: Gizela, be patient. And you, Benjy, be a man to the end of your life because this is your duty and your right as well. Brush your teeth, wash your hands; even when you are a grown-up defend your convictions, brush your teeth, wash your ears, protect the values which are the most precious wealth transmitted from generation to generation. What if your father should go, if he leaves you everything and even more . . .

BENJAMIN *(trying to remove his father's palm from the top of his head):* But Mommy . . .

HENRY: And you, Gizela, be a woman. Do not depart from this under any circumstances. Had your grandpa had the time to leave me any directives regarding bringing you up . . . but after all, I know what he could have thought in his last hour . . . He was a very good man but a little irresponsible. Yes, Gizela, be a woman always, train your character. One day you will be a mother. I know you wanted to be a boy . . . Benjy, don't fidget so much—after all, my words are for you too. It makes no sense if someone talks very wisely but his breath is foul. Such, unfortunately, is our contemporary world. Anyway, at all times one must think not only of oneself . . . One must struggle with oneself. My children, one must place greater demands on oneself than on others . . . You are the people of the future . . .

BENJAMIN: Easy to say that . . .

HENRY: Don't be so glib, child. You will not even notice when you are a new man. Can't you sit still for a minute? Wash your ears, Benjy, brush your hair, fold up your pants. And you, Gizela, don't allow yourself to be outdistanced, you are a girl but everything lies open to you . . .

BENJAMIN: Mommy . . .

HENRY: The poor thing . . . in her there is a struggle between the new and the old. Do not seek personal gain in anything. I can leave you nothing apart from my name. Remember, Benjy, that no Hoopoe ever stained himself . . .

BENJAMIN *(laughs):* Hoopoe, what Hoopoe didn't stain himself?

HENRY *(realizing suddenly that he has blundered and said something idiotic)*: My head is splitting ... I'm afraid I'm going to be sick ... I shall throw up everything. Gizela, hand me that bucket ...

GIZELA *hands it to him and supports his head.* HENRY *attempts to be sick but without success. He struggles for a long time, his head hidden in the vessel. He talks with his head inside the bucket. His voice comes out muffled but clear.*

I'm going. I shall leave you nothing but my name. On your father's side, Benjy, you are the inheritor of those values which your grandpa had developed in himself. That grandpa who was unable to finish what he wished to say because a tragic configuration of causes had, like one of the Fates, cut the thread of his life. Whose works were the fruit of above-average spiritual values. Remember, Benjy, no Lavender stained his hands and your grandpa marched with his head held high ... *(He is sick and then resumes.)* Be a man, Benjy. When you are on a bus give up your seat to the elderly. What is a man in our times? Neither a protector nor a provider ... Defend your convictions with your head held high ... Always be an optimist ... Fly toward the sun ... And you, Gizela, always be a woman ... *(He is sick again.)* Wash your hands, Benjy, guard your post, never change your name. Your name includes everything that your forebears have collected and with your name you will transmit these values to your successors. What an odd custom we have nowadays in this country. Was there ever a time when a louse wanted to call itself an eagle? A rat call itself a lark, a mouse a cat, a cat a dog ... ? *(He laughs bitterly, his head still inside the bucket.)* Changes of name are fashionable, but this involves a lot of cowardice, vanity, and stupidity ... What is a man without a name? With a name changed he is like a man without a face, without a past and without ancestors . . . Sometimes when an ancestor stains himself with a terrible crime one can justify such a change, though even Bormann's son has not repudiated his father's name nor has Goering's daughter nor had Hitler's sister nor Mussolini's son. Who then should repudiate his name since even the child of a man responsible for genocide bears his father's name? Oh, my children, why does Foot want to be called Head, why does Fishman call himself Eaglestone and why does Rat become Pratt? In a free country where love and sympathy rule let Cock remain Cock, let Rat remain Rat and let Hoopoe remain Hoopoe. And although your grandpa was a mere foundling whom a gypsy picked up on a railway station platform . . .

HENRY *is sick and then resumes.* EVE *enters with a bowl of soup. She places the bowl on the table and leaves the room without taking any notice of her husband and children.*

BENJAMIN, *who has meanwhile extricated himself from his father's grip, approaches the table, having left the cage with the white mice on a side table.*

BENJAMIN: Daddy! Soup . . .

HENRY *(his face still hidden in the bucket):* . . . one has to know, Benjy, how not to lose face.

BENJAMIN: Don't worry, Daddy, everything will turn out all right . . .

EVE *returns to set the table and then goes out.*

GIZELA *supports her father's head and moves the bucket away. She takes a handkerchief out of her pocket and carefully wipes his face.*

GIZELA: The poor thing! How do such thoughts get into his empty head? Probably he overfed himself on his pitiful past. I told Mommy, "Don't push so much into him, it's already coming out of his ears." But you know Mommy! "I must push everything I can into his gut—I'll stuff into him all of life's gruel and fuel," and so on and so on. You know Mommy, Benjy, don't you? She has had her way.

BENJAMIN: Daddy's throwing up.

EVE: Soup's on the table.

She pours out the soup. They all sit down and eat the soup in silence.

Today, Henry, we have your favorite soup.

HENRY: Cucumber?

EVE: Tomato.

GIZELA: Mommy, you forgot that Daddy loves cucumber soup most of all.

EVE: You're wrong, child. I've known Father for some little while now. He always delighted in tomato soup. I remember when he was courting me my mother always used to say, "Henry, today we have your favorite soup," and she would joke that "the gentleman will get caught by this soup." And he was.

GIZELA *(laughs heartily)*: Oh, Mommy, what primitive times those were. Who today would think of catching a man or a boy with soup—and tomato soup at that?

BENJAMIN: Don't count your chickens before they're hatched.

GIZELA: Mommy, tell that child not to talk gibberish.

HENRY *is eating the soup in silence. He is using a fork but no one has noticed.*

EVE: Have you told Father about the changes we have all experienced since the last war? About the political system in which we live?

GIZELA: Yes.

HENRY: Never underestimate the cooking. Don't underestimate sauces! English cooking is like the cooking of cannibals because food weighs down their spirit—and what about German cooking? Those sauces, those meats, those pastries! Piedmontese cooking is best.

EVE: But you could have told Daddy a few things about communism, capitalism, socialism, stalinism, dogmatism, and revisionism.

GIZELA: Recently I read quite interesting things about that. *Eve's Madness* is probably the last word in these matters.

EVE: And who wrote that?

GIZELA: A Frenchman, a poet. In his view, evolution of love leads to the Age of the Tandem Couple . . .

BENJAMIN: The age of the tandem? He must have got it wrong . . . the age of the tandem is past.

GIZELA: Mommy, tell him to stop his smart talk. We're not talking about bicycles but about the couple that is formed by man and woman.

EVE: Benjy, leave us for a minute. This topic is not for your ears.

BENJAMIN *leaves.*

GIZELA: He says that our age is the age of Eve.

EVE: And who is this Eve?

GIZELA: That's his wife . . . He says that the time of the couple is at hand.

HENRY: Just as before there was competition between blood and iron.

GIZELA: The age of labor in which man and woman create and preserve love.

EVE: It's so very nice of this man. The French are really so charming. Even ideologically.

GIZELA: Yes, he's a charming elderly man. Really charming. Listen to what he says about communism. *(She takes a notebook out of her pocket, looks through it and reads.)* "Let's take the problem of communism . . ."

EVE: Henry, listen, this is something for you.

GIZELA: "Not so long ago people talked of communism as though it were something very distant and today there are people who talk about communism as of a thing very close and even give dates: the year 1980. The year 1980 is very close.

Each one of us tries to imagine how and what things will look like then. Perhaps falsely and subjectively. But as far as I am concerned—says the poet—subjectivism rests on the fact that I imagine communism . . .

BENJAMIN *(knocks)*: May I come in to finish my soup?

EVE: Yes, but don't interrupt us.

BENJAMIN *sits down at the table and dutifully drinks his soup.*

GIZELA: "I imagine communism as a society whose basic cell will be a couple of close, happy people loving each other."

EVE: That's charming. Well, really, I never expected . . .

BENJAMIN, *who was listening with attention to Gizela's last words, cannot control himself any more and bursts out laughing. However, his mouth is full of tomato soup with rice. He spatters the soup not only on himself but also on* GIZELA *and his father. He is choking and cannot catch his breath. Only after a considerable pause he calms down and wipes his tears with his thumbs.*

BENJAMIN: The idiot. Oh, Mommy, Mommy, o mamma mia, what is this idiotic girl talking about . . .

HENRY *has put aside his fork and is now picking a tooth with his finger.*

EVE: And you're really not interested in anything. Neither in your children's future nor in me. All you care about is eating your soup and having a night's sleep.

HENRY *(interrupting his tooth-picking)*: Darling, you're unjust to the boy.

EVE: What did you say?

HENRY: Benjy, leave us for a minute.

BENJAMIN *leaves.*

Indeed the boy made a mistake in not swallowing the soup. He had his mouth full and that is what caused the incident.

On the other hand, it seems to me that he was right in his evaluative judgment regarding what Gizela, following that charming Frenchman, just told us. Darling, let's for example take the case of the cell which is supposed to be the basic cell of society. I'm not surprised that the child was amused by the babbling of the old intellectual. You see, children have something like a sharpened instinct in their evaluation of phenomena. Children are the only realists on earth. The true cell which will in future form the basis of society will be the family and not this gentleman's tandem couple. That is to say: the husband, the wife, the children, the mother-in-law, the grandfather, and even the uncle. It's all very well to sing about the couple, of course it's more comfortable when there is a couple, but the couple is not the soul, the couple is only an egotistic association and it's not good idealizing the thing . . . the age of the couple! Benjy was right to laugh at Gizela, although he should have done it after swallowing his cucumber soup. I too found it difficult to restrain myself. Gizela is a young miss, she is seventeen, so she can, without any ill effects upon her mind and organism, transcribe into her diary these lyrical raptures. Benjy, come here and finish your soup.

BENJAMIN *enters, sits down dutifully at the table and solemnly consumes his soup.*

You see, my boy, never laugh at adults when your mouth is full of soup. Retain your laughter until you've swallowed it.

BENJAMIN *(swallows and says solemnly):* Yes, Daddy.

HENRY: And if this gentleman had eleven, or at least four, children, he would sing the age of the couple in a different manner. Well, really, what a load of rubbish.

EVE: Don't cry, Gizela, you can see Father is joking. Wipe the soup out of your eyes.

BENJAMIN: Don't cry, Gizela, I didn't mean to hurt you. Stop whimpering, I'll give you a white mouse, shall I?

GIZELA: You always make fun of everything. What's wrong with this man imagining communism like this?

BENJAMIN: Don't you know, you goose, that the age of the couple already existed in paradise? Monsieur had forgotten about such details as artificial manure, heavy industry, electrification, social security, shorter working hours, and chemistry. The French are very charming and want to settle everything either in bed or around the bed. That's their national virtue: with them politics, art, and all their literature happens either in bed or under the bed . . .

EVE: Benjy, will you leave the table at once.

HENRY: Let him finish the soup.

EVE: How can a child at his age . . . the things he hears in the street and on the bus . . . so many drunkards everywhere . . . He watches television programs in secret.

BENJAMIN: So what do you want me to do? Feed myself on silly little rhymes in books with colored pictures? Where imbeciles write about dwarfs and dwarfs write about imbeciles? My God, things have come to a pretty pass in the world of adults. I tell you, Gizela, at school you hear a lot of double talk. The priest tells you about angels and the biology teacher tells you about protein. One's head reels . . . And now this one comes along with his age of the couple . . . while under the bed there's probably "that third one" like in all the plays and films.

GIZELA *bursts into tears. She spatters her soup not only on* BENJAMIN *but also on her father. Hurt, she runs out of the room.*

EVE: Gizela, please bring in the roast.

A FAT MAN *appears in the doorway, bows, goes over to* EVE, *bows once more and kisses her hand.*

Oh, it's you. I've completely forgotten . . . The school friend?

FAT MAN *(bowing):* Yes, a school friend. I received your telegram yesterday . . .

EVE: Well, as a matter of fact, my husband has come to his senses . . . but do . . . please sit down . . . here, next to me . . . Benjy, say "How do you do."

BENJAMIN *stops eating, bows politely to* FAT MAN. *The* FAT MAN *holds him under the chin and scrutinizes his face.* HENRY *is feverishly looking for something in his pockets. He draws out a roll of bandage. He is concentrating and his expression is serious.*

FAT MAN: The image of his father.

EVE: Would you like some soup? Here everything's as usual. Henry is slowly recovering his senses.

FAT MAN *(holding* BENJAMIN *under the chin):* Yes, please, thank you very much. You like tomato soup, sonny, I can see it in your eyes. And how is school, my dear sir? The very image of father.

GIZELA *enters smiling: there are traces of tears on her face.*

EVE: Gizela, wash the soup out of your eyes. I'm awfully sorry; just a moment ago we had a little incident at table. As you know, with children . . . My daughter. Say "How do you do." This is Father's friend, a school colleague.

HENRY *looks carefully at* FAT MAN *and then slowly begins to wrap the bandage around his head.*

FAT MAN: The image of his father. *(He lays down his spoon and holds* GIZELA *under the chin.)* And how is school? Have you got a boyfriend?

BENJAMIN: May I get back to the soup?

EVE: Yes, please do.

BENJAMIN *sits down dutifully and finishes his soup.*

We're waiting for Henry's mother. Perhaps memories of

schooldays will prove stronger. One has to get at the roots. I don't really know myself. Mother sees him with a ribbon in his hair. She says he had curls. What do you think about that?

HENRY *has finished bandaging his head. Now he again looks as he did in Tableau Four of Act Two, but this time his ears stick out from behind the bandage. This apparent detail will make possible the final development of dramatic action.* FAT MAN *stops eating his soup, smiles and winks knowingly toward* HENRY *and then leans over and whispers something in Henry's ear.* HENRY *sits motionless.* FAT MAN *bursts out laughing, pulls* HENRY *by the ear like a small boy, then returns to his soup. After a while* HENRY *puts down his napkin, gets up, and without saying a word leaves the room.* EVE *follows him with her eyes, opens her mouth . . .*

THE END